Carol Engler was an award-winning newspaper reporter before she went into real estate 39 years ago. Story writing will always be her first love. She is happily married with five gorgeous grandkids. Carol still actively advocates for children with special needs.

For Aaron and Lauren who taught me so much about love and family. And for Michael who happily joined in on all the craziness!

Carol Engler

AARON'S STORY

ONE WRONG TURN

AUSTIN MACAULEY PUBLISHERS™

LONDON · CAMBRIDGE · NEW YORK · SHARJAH

A CIP catalogue record for this title is available from the British Library.

ISBN 9781528990721 (Paperback)
ISBN 9781787107366 (ePub e-book)

www.austinmacauley.com

First Published (2021)
Austin Macauley Publishers Ltd
25 Canada Square
Canary Wharf
London
E14 5LQ

Chapter 1
The Beginning

One of my best girlfriends told me to start at the very beginning. How does one start from the beginning when the middle and ending are what matters?

My son, Aaron, had so many mental health and emotional issues, I had a difficult time keeping track of them. Throw in a father who spent 25 years 'living in Egypt on the River Denial', insisting that Aaron was 'all boy', add in Aaron's younger sister whose face was smashed in when she was physically assaulted by him, and then top it off with a workaholic Jewish mother who would sneak back to the office just seeking to hang on to the very last bit of sanity she had. Now that's a dysfunctional family on steroids – and it was mine.

I was born to be a Jewish mother. Every person in and around my world knows they were going to get a healthy dose of Jewish Motherhood from me – whether they wanted it or not.

Don and I were married for ten fabulous fun-filled years before I became pregnant (it took me that long to figure out from where babies came). When I got over the initial shock and finally shared the happy news with him, he said he wasn't ready to be a father and walked out of my real estate office. I burst into tears and sulked the rest of the day.

The following morning, I was greeted by two dozen red roses – and a note saying something to the effect that "we can get through this". That should have been my first clue about our mutually shared doubt.

At 33, I knew that if you didn't like your house, you could move into something different. You didn't like your dog – you could give it away to a new loving family. You didn't like your spouse – you could go out with the old and in with the new. What do you do with a baby if you decided you didn't like motherhood after all? Was there a way to put that thing back from where it came?

Don and I never really discussed the issue of children. We were having way too much fun being the happy couple. We would work at our respective offices until 6 p.m. every night Monday through Thursday, go out for a lovely dinner together and then head back to our offices at 8 p.m. We would continue working until 10 p.m. at which time we would go home and sleep in until 10 the next morning. Who wanted a baby to interfere with this perfect world?

I nervously called my aunt in Florida who reassured me that children had a way of 'inching their way into your heart'. I honestly didn't believe her but thought it would be one of those 'wait and see' moments.

I put on no less than 60 pounds with this pregnancy because I knew I was eating for two – right? Two entrees, two appetizers, two desserts at EVERY SINGLE MEAL. I was really liking this license to eat.

At one of my monthly check ups, I was waiting in the doctor's office with the other patients and commented loudly for the whole office to hear that "pregnancy sucks!" At 200-plus pounds in the 109-degree Yuma summer heat, I didn't have a lot of nice things to say about the weather or my pregnancy – or anything else for that matter.

Apparently, I upset one of the newly pregnant young "mothers to be" who burst into tears and told my doctor how mean and awful I was. I was quickly relegated to the last appointment of the day at the clinic so I would no longer come into contact with any more of the new mothers-to-be – those SISSIES.

August 1, 1986 arrived nice and steamy, humid and hot. I was right in the middle of negotiating a purchase contract with a seller, Lore, when it was time to go to the hospital. I was scheduled to be induced within the hour, and I hadn't been home to pack my bags. I told Lore (who eventually let me adopt her as my second mother) that I needed to get to the hospital NOW, and would she PLEASE hurry up and sign the contract so I could leave and take care of this annoying business called childbirth. She said she would wait until I was finished having the baby and would come back and sign at a later date.

Wrong answer. I told her I was going to have this baby IN MY OFFICE right then and there and it would be all her fault. Needless to say, she signed, and I dashed off to the local hospital to get my drugs and have this baby.

My OB-GYN's wife was my Lamaze coach. I asked myself – who needed Lamaze when you were such good personal friends with the delivering doctor and his wife? Surely, he would give me drugs the moment I walked through the hospital door.

WRONG! No one told me that they don't give you pain killers until you start to dilate. Why was that such a national secret that only the president of the United States (or his wife) knew?

My Lamaze coach and I started doing our Lamaze breathing together like there was no tomorrow. Every time the fetal monitor would bleep instead of blip, she would page her husband and make him come down to the labor/delivery ward to see if everything was still OK.

After about the fifth false alarm, he told her to stop dragging him down there until it was time for me to actually deliver. She asked him pointedly, "And just how many children did you personally spit out?"

He said he had delivered thousands of babies. She persisted, asking him repeatedly how many babies he had personally HAD. "I rest my case," was her final retort.

After eight hours of unbearable labor pains, I decided to get off the hospital gurney and go home. I had had enough of this nonsense and unmitigated agony. How could labor pains be so barbaric in this modern world?

I don't really know to this day if the doctor just got sick and tired of me or his wife (or both of us together), but the next thing I knew I was being prepped for a C-section. Off to La La Land I went with a smile on my face – finally.

Don and Carol – "pre-children era".

Chapter 2
I Wanted a Girl!

When I woke up the next day, I asked the nurse what I had. "Demerol and some other drug concoction," she said happily.

"No," I responded. "Not what drugs did I have. What kind of baby did I have?"

She said it was a boy and all I remember saying was, "Shit. I wanted a baby woman."

Aaron Casey Engler entered the world at just under ten pounds. Don said he came out smoking a cigar. The second thing he said was, "Oh my God, look at the size of his paws!"

I was a busy real estate agent so just having had a baby was no reason for me to stop working. Those were the days before cell phones, so I told all my clients, customers, friends and enemies to call me anytime at the hospital's maternity ward. I was a one-person office in those days, and I was so busy that the nurses' station was fielding my many phone calls and actually taking messages for me.

After a second day of THAT nonsense, my OB-GYN doctor, doing his rounds, sternly reminded me this was a hospital – not a real estate office – and could I please lay off the phone calls. No sense of humor with that one.

Aaron's newly appointed Godmother, Mary Beth, stayed with us the first ten days of his life. Don and I were terrified of this little baby that needed to be fed, changed and bathed on a regular basis. Neither of us had ever been around any babies (much less a new one). We truly had no idea what to expect or what we were supposed to actually do.

At one point, after Mary Beth 'abandoned us', I asked Don if he wanted to go out to dinner and he said yes. We were just stepping out the door when I stopped and said, "Oh my God, we can't go to Chretins for dinner!" Don said, "That's right – you like El Charro's better. OK. We can go there," as he continued walking out of the house.

I hollered at him as he was heading to the car, "We can't go anywhere – we have a baby in the house!!!"

Scary beginning.

Chapter 3
I Got My Girl!

Fast-forward two years – I was pregnant with our daughter, Lauren Elizabeth. I was in a 'Hollywood state of mind' and named her after Lauren Bacall and Elizabeth Taylor.

During my pregnancy with Aaron, I was tossing my cookies the entire nine months. Lauren's pregnancy was a piece of cake! I have a great picture of me at eight months as a pregnant nun/undertaker. We sure had some amazing Halloween parties back then.

I wanted Lauren to be born on December 7, 1988, 'a day that would live in infamy'. Don was not as excited about that as I, so we settled on a planned C-section the morning before. (Had we known she would turn out to be such a force of nature, we would have kept December 7, 1988.)

We had been explaining to Aaron for months that he was getting a baby sister – he was so excited…until he saw what a baby sister was. When he was brought to the hospital to meet her for the first time, he took one look at her and then insisted to everybody in my hospital room that we should take him home RIGHT NOW…and leave her there.

Chapter 4
Aaron Did What?

Back to the saga of Aaron at age two – I remember telling Don that I was concerned there was something wrong with our son. While I couldn't exactly put my finger on it, I knew that the other children in pre-school/day care were not acting like him. I don't remember the other mothers talking about their two-year-olds pulling out knives from the kitchen drawer and waving them.

Don told me, that since I had grown up with only sisters and no brothers, how could I know how a young boy was supposed to act? He chalked up these unusual actions to Aaron being 'all boy'.

I was only his mother – what did I know?

About two years after that conversation I decided to purchase a mail-order 'GI Joe of America' doll for Aaron. It never arrived.

Being the patient, mild mannered mother that I was, I sent a scathing letter to Hasbro, asking them how could they cash my check and then not send my son the doll he was so anxious to own? What kind of United States' business would do this to this poor deserving four-year-old boy?

Well, Hasbro clearly agreed with me because two weeks later some 40 GI Joe dolls arrived at the house with a letter from Hasbro apologizing for the breakdown in communication. I was so excited to show my son that when his mother meant business, the world responded!!! I was just so darn proud of myself.

The next day when I came home from work, I was shocked to see that every single GI Joe doll had been smashed into smithereens. I was so upset, I was speechless (and trust me that is a very rare event). I asked Aaron, what happened to the dolls I had been so delighted in obtaining on his behalf.

He simply said, "My brain made me do it."

A few weeks later, I noticed that the brick BBQ in front of our house had been partially destroyed with a large rock. There were pieces of it scattered on the front porch.

I asked Aaron if he knew anything about the damage. He told me for the second time in two weeks, "My brain made me do it."

The final straw came a few weeks later when I noticed a small river of liquid seeping out from under the door of our garage. I went inside to check it out and knew immediately what had happened with just one whiff. My parents' entire collection of Kachina Doll decanters had been smashed into pieces and all that strong liquor had run out of the garage and down the driveway.

When I got into the house, I asked Aaron if he knew anything about it. For the third time, he told me, "My brain made me do it."

At this point I was absolutely certain that something was 'wrong' with our son. His dad, forever living a life of denial, told me I was overreacting AGAIN, and that Aaron was 'all boy'.

It was around this time that his father bought him the movie RoboCop. Obviously we were not aware of its PG rating. Aaron apparently memorized the most important part of the movie because one morning he stalked into the kitchen just like RoboCop. He trooped upstairs to see his grandmother who had just arrived for a visit. In a serious stance with his feet spread apart, and two play guns in his hands, he proceeded to tell everyone within earshot to "come with me, motherfucker, or there will be trouble!"

Absolute dead silence in our household at that moment. After an embarrassing pause that did NOT refresh, someone shouted, "What did he say?"

Interestingly, Aaron's speech was not quite where it needed to be at that stage of his life. He would mumble and

15

not always communicate clearly. But in this case, Aaron's response was to repeat exactly what he had said – just louder and clearer. Why he was able to enunciate those words so clearly at that exact moment is still a mystery to this day! I knew, right then and there, what my mother-in-law thought of my pathetic parenting skills.

Chapter 5
Let the Fun and Games Begin

I was delighted (and relieved), when Aaron was old enough to enroll in kindergarten and then made it to the first grade at Ronald Reagan Elementary School. This was Yuma's very first charter school in those days, and only cookie cutter children were suited for this particular kind of educational environment. Too bad, I didn't understand that very important fact at the time!

I knew we were in trouble one morning after I had dropped Aaron off at school. The principal flagged me down, jumped into my car and sternly told me to "drive".

He angrily asked me, "Why is Aaron sniffing the classroom chairs and drawing phallic symbols during classroom time?" What kind of mother was I and, clearly, in what psycho home environment was this child being raised?

Whatever on earth made him think I had a clue???

I knew for quite some time that Aaron had a 'missing link' somewhere but doctor after doctor told us he was just fine! I took him to an allergy doctor because he was always clearing his throat. I took him to multiple psychiatrists, psychologists and social workers to try to understand why he did such crazy things. Aaron spit at his regular pediatrician who was not thrilled to see him as many times as he did – but still no answers, until…

One day in the kitchen, my niece piped up out of the blue, "I know what's wrong with Aaron. He has Tourette Syndrome." I asked her why she was so certain of something that multiple doctors in three different states couldn't diagnose or even understand. She said she knew it was

Tourette's because her boyfriend, Bobby, did the same things. "Haven't you noticed all those quirky and little squeaking noises he makes around you?"

And here all this time I just thought I made him nervous – well, duh!

After going to the library (those were the olden days before the internet) and reading about Tourette's, I knew my niece was spot on. The books I read described everything Aaron did to a 'T'. Sniffing chairs, barking, involuntary tics such as repetitive eye-blinking, facial movements, shoulder shrugging, throat clearing, coughing, snorting – it was all there.

Tourette Syndrome (TS) is a common, inherited neurodevelopmental disorder characterized by multiple involuntary movements and sometimes uncontrollable vocal sounds, all referred to as tics. These tics characteristically wax and wane, and can only be suppressed temporarily.

The disorder is named for Dr Gilles de la Tourette (1857–1904), a French neurologist who first diagnosed the disease in a noble woman in 1885.

The symptoms of TS generally appear before 18 years of age. It can affect people of all ethnic groups and males are affected three to four times more than females. This disorder affects one's communication skills and social behavior.

Symptoms begin in early childhood and last throughout a lifetime. They start at the top and work their way done…headshaking, rapid eye blinking that leads to nose twitching or grimacing. It is not uncommon for TS kids to continuously clear their throats, cough, sniff, grunt, yelp, bark or shout. We had Aaron treated for two years for asthma…that he didn't have.

One of the most misunderstood aspects of Tourette's is coprolalia, where people involuntarily shout obscenities. This behavior is extremely rare, but it gets the most media attention.

There are a number of other 'spectrum disorders' that are associated with Tourette Syndrome. These include Asperger's Syndrome, Obsessive Compulsive Disorder (OCD),

Attention Deficit Disorder (ADD with and without hyperactivity), various learning disabilities and sleep disorders. And Aaron had them all!

It is estimated that as many as 12% or 7.5 million people in this country suffer from Tourette Syndrome. People suffering from TS have a larger percentage of 'white matter' in their frontal lobes. Their brains have an increased number of Dopamine receptors which manufacture more dopamine than the synapses can handle.

This is what creates the involuntary movements, impulsivity and lack of inner control i.e. the civilized part of the brain keeps your mouth from blurting out what you think. "I hate the way you wear your hair" could be an example. Now you might THINK this, but you wouldn't blurt it out to a total stranger. Aaron did not have that kind of control. He once told a pregnant woman he hated the baby that was in her stomach!

Asperger's Syndrome was first described in the 1940s by Viennese pediatrician Hans Asperger, who observed autism-like behaviors and difficulties with social and communication skills in boys who had normal intelligence and language development. It differs from classic autism in that it is less severe with the absence of language delays.

Attention Deficit Hyperactivity Disorder is the most commonly diagnosed mental disorder of children. They may be hyperactive and unable to control their impulses.

READY!

FIRE!

AIM!

OOPS!

© Parkaire Consultants, Inc. 1989

Their inability to pay attention interferes with both school and home life. These kids grow up to have extreme difficulty in managing their time, being organized and setting goals. They may also have significant problems later in life with relationships, self-esteem and addiction.

A friend of mine, who was a Registered Nurse, suggested I contact the National Tourette Syndrome Association (TSA) in New York so I could educate myself about Aaron's neurological disorder. The staff members there became my new best friends (whether they wanted it or not!)

At one point, I was calling them so often the head gal nicely asked me to stop contacting them with new questions every single day, and to please get in touch with the Arizona chapter for more local and timely assistance. Who knew?

I was absolutely blessed to have Molly, from the Tucson chapter, fly to Yuma and help save what little was left of my sanity. She explained to Don, Aaron and me what was happening in Aaron's brain and why he did such crazy, out of the ordinary antics all the time.

Molly explained that the main culprit for Tourette Syndrome is dopamine – one of several important chemicals in the brain. According to the National TSA, abnormalities in dopamine transmission have a direct link to this and other neurological disorders. Dopamine, we learned, was also directly related to his onset of tics.

Chapter 6
Who Knew?

Once we knew what was 'wrong' with Aaron, I discovered that the National Tourette Syndrome Association was hosting a conference in Burbank, Calif. I grabbed my trusty twin sister, Roni, and headed over to California to learn more about this new, life-altering intrusion. Was I ever in for a big surprise!

Watching and listening to Aaron's tics alone, is one thing. Being in a room with a 1000-plus people twitching, grunting, barking and just being their normal selves was a bit overwhelming for the first time…to say the least.

When the announcer welcomed everybody to the conference, his first question was, "What are we all here for?" I'm thinking to say something profound – like new knowledge or some new discovery to minimize the effects of this dreaded neurological disorder.

Wrong answer! The first cry out of everyone's mouth was, "We're here to TIC!" And tic, they all did!!!

There was a relatively unknown actress at the time named Neve Campbell who came up on stage and spoke about her brother's challenge with Tourette's. I had never heard of her before but was thoroughly impressed with her incredible knowledge, care and concern for her younger brother. She went on to become quite an accomplished actress. She has appeared as a major character in 'Skyscraper', 'House of Cards', 'Party of Five' and 'Scream' and this is just a partial list.

I had so much new information thrown at me. To say I was overwhelmed was an understatement. How could this many people in the same place have what my son had...and yet, they seemed to have found ways to cope with it all.

The question, I nervously stood up and asked, was whether I should listen to and obey my son's second grade teacher or ignore her and simply pay attention to my own gut instincts. She wanted him to be a regular student and go on field trips and do activities with the rest of the class. I didn't know what to do – try to help him fit in with his peers or acknowledge his limitations? After all, wasn't his teacher the expert? Didn't she know how to work with and handle ALL types of children?

The group's response was loud and clear – LISTEN TO MY KID! I learned that day that I was his only advocate – the teachers, students and school personnel could not get inside his head. I was the only one able to understand what he was going through. It fell solely on my shoulders to help ease his way.

I recall, I was eating dinner by myself at a restaurant at this same conference, when a total stranger came up to me and asked if I was here for the Tourette Syndrome conference. "Of course," I said; because my son had been newly diagnosed and I was here to learn more about how I could help him cope.

The man looked me right in the eye and asked, "Well, what about you? What are you doing for your Tourette's?" What??? How dare he???

I asked him, not so nicely, why he thought I was the one in my family with Tourette's. After all, I had blamed everything in our family on Don – alcoholism, depression, multiple suicide attempts by family members, etc. Who did he think he was to tell me Aaron's disorder came from my side of the family???

He proceeded to ask me if I ever looked in the mirror and saw my mouth twitching ALL the time? He then asked did I realize I was being hyperactive and obsessively compulsive in the way I placed and ate the food on my plate?

How dare he???

I left the restaurant in a huff and told Roni what that insensitive bastard had just told me! Of course, I denied everything…until Roni and I had a heart to heart 'come to Jesus' meeting later that night.

She reminded me (nicely) that she and I BOTH had tics when we were around the age of five years old. At that time our mother called them 'sheckles'. We would shrug our shoulders, make noises and unexpectedly do 'plies' all the time – who knew???

Then we spoke of our dad who was ALWAYS clearing his throat and constantly picking at his fingernails. And no story would be complete without my own Obsessive-Compulsive Disorder (OCD) details when I was ten years old.

OCD is characterized by unreasonable thoughts and fears (obsessions) that lead to repetitive behaviors (compulsions). Unfortunately, this condition cannot be cured.

I remember lining up my dolls in my bedroom in the same order every night before I went to sleep. God help the poor soul who dared to move them! I would also wash my hands over and over again until they bled profusely, and I constantly suffered from open sores.

And then, there was the time when I was 13 years old and looked up an assortment of diseases in the World Book Encyclopedia. I had convinced myself I was suffering from each and every one of them – rabies, tetanus, bubonic plague – you name it, I thought I had it!

OCD and Tourette's are part of the autism spectrum. This is a neurological and developmental disorder that affects one's communication and behavior. Symptoms begin in early childhood and last throughout a lifetime. It affects how a person acts and interacts with others, communicates and learns. This disorder includes Asperger's Syndrome and other pervasive developmental disorders that are considered part of that same autism spectrum.

I went home from the Tourette's conference as Yuma's new and only 'expert' on this disorder. I went to the newspaper and asked them to write a story on Aaron and his Tourette's. They did a great article on him when he was eight years old.

Credit: The Yuma Daily Sun

From then on, I became the 'go-to' mother for anyone in Yuma with a twitch. I started a local support group for the 'as-yet-to-be' diagnosed sufferers. Who knew there were so many people in my small community suffering from this as yet unknown disorder with no one to help? Not on my watch!

I became the poster girl for advocating for children with special needs in my hometown. Mothers would call me and ask me to help diagnose their children. Wives called me to see how they could get their husbands diagnosed. Even my eye doctor called to tell me one of his employee's had a son with symptoms similar to Aaron's. Could I meet with them and help?

One of the most memorable jokes about Aaron's Tourette's was the time we had a husband and wife over to our house for dinner one night. Aaron was upstairs in the loft watching television or playing a game. He started barking as that had become his latest and greatest tic. These tics wax and wane, changing constantly. Each day may bring forth an entirely new and different tic!

So here Don and I were – talking and obliviously eating dinner – when one of our guests asked us what kind of dog we owned. Without missing a beat, we both said out loud in unison, "Oh, that's just Aaron," and kept right on eating without missing a bite. I guess we were simply getting used to Aaron being Aaron, with his litany of different tics.

Chapter 7
Can You Say Columbine?

Don and I agreed that Aaron would be transferred to Valley Horizon, a 'regular' public school to start the second grade. I remember someone called our transfer meeting 'the mother of all IEP's (Individualized Education Plan)' with 27 people in attendance. These federally mandated plans are developed by local schools for students who require specific aspects of special education. This was an attendance-setting record of the century for one IEP!

Joining us at the meeting was Aaron's local psychiatrist, the Crane School District's psychologists, both the outgoing and incoming heads of the special education department, along with multitudes of teachers from both schools. Molly Senor of the Arizona chapter of the National TSA came from Tucson to describe the educational aides that Aaron would need in his new school. I think even the school janitor joined in.

Apparently, Aaron's reputation from his previous school preceded him because when I spoke to the principal of the new school and explained that we planned to transfer Aaron to her school – all she said was, "Damn, I have to take him. You're in my district!"

The ultimate trade-off for the school accepting my son was the principal's insistence that I accept the role as president of their PTA. Heck – why not? I don't mind being president of anything for which I don't have to campaign!

Things went merrily along for about a month until, finally, Valley Horizon gave me the needed validation that I was not the only questionable loon in my family!!!

I clearly remember when Aaron's teacher at that time called the house and spoke to Don. She flat out told him she was concerned that there was something wrong with Aaron. That comment definitely got his goat because he sarcastically asked her, "And when did you become a board-certified psychiatrist?"

Her comment was stellar and spot on – "I have 30 other kids in my classroom and there is definitely something wrong with yours!"

Hard to believe but the other kids in the classroom were not ALWAYS blurting out words and obscenities, touching classmates exactly three times on their body parts, etc. etc. Hello – is anyone home in that brain of his?

In the meantime, I was having a ball being the school's PTA president – we had all kinds of fun events, teacher appreciation lunches and even an interesting meeting about the newest rage – the concept of introducing computers to our school.

I use the word 'interesting' because it was at this PTA meeting that the computer proponent was touting how effective the new safeguards were to block young kids from accessing porn on the new computers. In less than two minutes, Aaron (who accompanied me to this particular meeting) accessed an adult porn site, yelling at everyone to come look at what he found.

Needless to say, the school did NOT purchase that computer software and the school administrators just chalked up this incident to yet another of Aaron's long list of infractions.

The second most distressing school incident (to put it mildly) was when Aaron picked up the young son of the future elementary school district superintendent and bounced him on his head in the hallway. Why Aaron did that, I will never know but I remember Don and I being called to the school for the umpteenth time to deal with yet another Aaron issue.

Laurie Doering was the assistant principal at the time and was always trying to bring out the better side of Aaron. But Laurie was eventually reduced to tears on this day because

Don was so dang MEAN to her and blaming all of Aaron's behavior on her and her school.

Yes, she tried to bring out Aaron's better side…but sometimes there just was no 'better side'.

Later, Don bragged that he reduced the assistant school principal to tears. WHO WOULD BE PROUD OF DOING SUCH A THING?

The powers that be, eventually decided that Aaron be placed in a combined second and third grade classroom with Mrs. Klee (who was up for sainthood during those years!)

To help in the transition, I insisted on having an in-service (an informational session) for both the teacher and students who came into contact with Aaron. Knowledge is power, so by explaining his unusual tics, barking noises, involuntary movements and grunts, I was hoping his classmates would be more understanding. Even though that is a lot to ask of second graders, some of them were even protective of Aaron, until…

Remember the Columbine shootings on April 20, 1999?

It took me literally years to teach Aaron how to socialize at school and say good morning to Mrs. Klee when he first walked into the classroom. We repeated it over and over and over again. My motto with Aaron was, 'Tell him, tell him again, keep telling him, and then tell him again what you just told him.'

But when it comes to blurting out the worst imaginable threat of that singular decade – "I'm going to go home to get my dad's guns and shoot everyone at this school." – well, THAT statement Aaron knew right off the cuff!

Could he have said anything worse than that at that particular time in history? Sadly, I think not.

***

The entire country was RAW with pain and emotion over what had just happened at Columbine, and that was when Aaron's brain put together the most chilling sentence possible!

Aaron was supposed to have a one-on-one aide with him at all unstructured school times, such as lunch and playground breaks. It was part and parcel of his Individualized Education Plan (which is something ALL handicapped/special students desperately need and should have at school.)

Apparently, the day following the Columbine tragedy, the aide didn't show up or he/she was missing in action. But the outcome was that Aaron's peers started teasing him and embarrassed him by pushing him backwards over another student, who was sprawled on all fours – right smack in front of a girl he had a crush on. What could be more embarrassing?

The police arrested Aaron at school and he was immediately expelled from Valley Horizon School. There is nothing more exciting than starting your day with a phone call from your kid's school telling you that your second grader has been arrested!

At this point, Don and I began our next Battle Royale. As a mother of a student, I totally agreed with the school's punishment given the circumstances of what had just occurred at Columbine. But, all Don saw was that the school deprived our son of his due process right to a public education.

I kept asking Don, why he would want Aaron to stay at a school that clearly did not want him there. The students ridiculed him, the teachers were frustrated to tears and the head of special education actually quit her post and retired early!

***

Chapter 8
First Residential
Treatment Center

After non-stop angst, fighting and negotiating with the school district, it was decided that Aaron would enroll at an RTC (residential treatment center) school in Phoenix. The only problem was Don refused to let Aaron sleep at the treatment center, so guess who was the lucky one who packed up her furniture, rented an apartment in Phoenix and then moved in with Aaron lock, stock and barrel? I can tell you this – it sure wasn't Don!!!

I was the one fearing for my own safety, and yet I was the parent moving to Phoenix with this volatile kid. It was a tough job, but someone had to do it!!!

I found an apartment in Scottsdale near the residential treatment center where I could drop him off every morning and then pick him up every day – sounds like a good plan, right?

Well, guess who closed that particular campus the first week we moved up there – you got it! So now I was tasked with driving him to the Glendale campus each and every day during rush hour. We're talking an hour and a half each way, twice a day, five days a week. Who drives three hours every single day to taxi a kid to a special needs school? Where was Uber or Lyft when I needed them?

What made this adventure so exhausting was that in addition to the 15 hour per week drive, I also drove Aaron home to Yuma every Friday evening and then back again to Scottsdale every Sunday like clockwork. Luckily, I was only in my 40s at that time and didn't really know how tired I was.

At this current stage in my life, I'm lucky I can drive safely back and forth to the grocery store. But back then, it was just a necessary part of my routine.

I had just purchased a new car for all this travel and was wanting to push it to the limit on the freeway between Yuma and Gila Bend. So, like an imbecile, I pressed the pedal to the metal and went 110 miles per hour just to see what this puppy could do. I only stayed at that speed a short time and then hit the brakes to follow the speed limit.

Leave it to Aaron to walk up to two uniformed Arizona Highway patrolmen in the coffee shop at our regular bathroom stop, and ask them if they wanted to arrest his mother for driving 110 miles per hour. I politely told the officers that Aaron was delusional, grabbed him by the ear, and stormed out of the restaurant.

Just another day in the life of being Aaron's mother!

At some point, it was decided that Aaron would fly back and forth to Phoenix because not only did we have my speeding to contend with, his latest and greatest verbal tic was to shout at the top of his lungs, "Look out!" and then try to grab the steering wheel of the car. I kept Aaron in the back seat but the thundering "Look Out" was getting rather stressful and dangerous, to say the least. At one point, I threatened to leave him on the side of the freeway if he kept doing this to me.

As if just having Aaron in Phoenix weren't difficult enough, I now was adding a trip to the Phoenix airport every Friday after school. I would escort Aaron to the gate (pre-2001), make sure he got on the plane and then let his father know what time to pick him up in Yuma.

Then I would hightail it back to Yuma and arrive around 8:30 pm at night totally frazzled, exhausted and emotionally drained having not seen our daughter for the previous five days.

I remember getting a forlorn phone call from Lauren while I was in Phoenix – she absolutely broke my heart! She said into the phone, "I see your (real estate) signs all over town and I know you're not here for me."

Try recovering from THAT conversation!

I lived this hectic crazy life for six months and if it weren't for two dear friends, I don't think I could have survived with my sanity. Kathy was living between Yuma and Phoenix at the time and she rescued me regularly with tennis and alcohol while Aaron was in school. So did my CPA friend, Craig McEntee. I don't know how I could have survived this ordeal without their constant attention and friendship.

During all this madness, my real estate office was pretty much running itself. I worked like a demon every Saturday and Sunday before heading back to Phoenix to pick Aaron up at the airport Sunday evening. And this was all before the time of cell phones and fancy wireless computers. Pay telephones were also becoming my best friend!

Then, my office manager of 19 years decided to leave my employ and open up her own real estate office. It was definitely time for the Phoenix Travelers to return home to Yuma once and for all!

Chapter 9
Second Residential Treatment Center

ARIZONA CHILDREN'S ASSOCIATION

After only being home for a short time, I unilaterally decided that Aaron should go to yet another RTC called Arizona Children's Association in Tucson. I can't recall the exact number this placement was but, as always, I had high hopes for success.

WRONG AGAIN!!!

The first time we met with the staff, the therapist told us that without a united front between father and mother, the child had an unlikely chance of success. We were doomed from the start.

Don wanted Aaron to live at home at all costs and I wanted Lauren and Carol to be safe! We were about as far away from a united front as the Middle East conflict.

Problems began almost immediately – Aaron was much larger in size and weight than the staff, so he was intimidating to say the least. Apparently, he was threatening the staff and actually beat up one of the counselors. I don't recall what happened to the counselor, but Aaron came back to Yuma with a black eye.

Within short order, Aaron was kicked out of this latest residential treatment center just before Christmas. I was beside myself yet again, and desperate for a safe haven for Lauren and myself.

When my dear friend and Aaron's 'second mother-in-command', Lisa Marie, and I went to Tucson to pick Aaron up and bring him home (God forbid Don should accompany and help me), I was taken aback by all the Christmas presents he was bringing home with him.

Apparently, Arizona Children's Association was founded in 1912 and opened in 1915 as a permanent home where orphaned and neglected children could be cared for and adopted. At some point in time, it became a residential treatment center for handicapped children with emotional problems.

The perception of orphaned and neglected children at Arizona Children's Association still remains today because Aaron came home that year with boxes and boxes of holiday goodies, presents and toys. I was floored. It seems the Tucson Fire Department and other local entities always 'adopted' the kids at Arizona Children's Association during the Christmas holiday and literally inundated these children with presents and holiday cheer.

Needless to say, Aaron already had a cache of Christmas and Chanukah goodies hidden for him at our house, so all these extra items were donated to Precious Treasures, a local charitable organization in nearby Somerton.

Chapter 10
Third Residential Treatment Center – Meridell

At the age of 10, Aaron was off to yet another residential treatment center – this time in Austin, Texas. It was called Meridell Achievement Center and it was a godsend for us.

Despite being diagnosed with a spectrum of brain, mental and neurological disorders, some piece was still missing from the puzzle. I couldn't put my finger on it – and neither could all the other numerous doctors, psychiatrists and therapists in Aaron's life.

Aaron was either drugged and slept all the time, or was extremely hyperactive, which resulted in his being both volatile AND violent.

Don and I had been scouring for treatment centers in Phoenix and either they wouldn't accept Aaron, or it was just not the right fit. I remember sitting at a Waffle House in Phoenix with my head in my hands, feeling hopeless, depressed and VERY unhappy. Why couldn't we find what was wrong and actually HELP our son???

My friend from Julian, Cynthia, unfortunately bore the brunt of my upset when she called me one day to ask me a simple question about the log cabin she was renting from us. I jumped all over her on the phone for bothering me with such a trivial matter when my whole world was crashing down around me. I just couldn't take this stress and pressure anymore!!!

After I had dumped on Cynthia, she called this psychiatrist friend of hers in Utah and explained what I was going through. Her friend asked Cynthia to think of the absolute worst day of her life. That, she said, is what Carol lives with each and every single day of HER life.

First, this Utah psychiatrist suggested we check out a new RTC in St George, Utah. So up to Utah, Don and I drove. For whatever reason, I cannot remember, we decided this was not a good fit for our son. That's when we were told by this same psychiatrist about Meridell Achievement Center in Austin, Texas. What a much-needed blessing, and it was about damn time!!!

During the several months Aaron was there, we learned he had what's called 'Complex Seizure Disorder' or what I simply called Epilepsy of the Brain. The doctor explained that Aaron's brain was having silent seizures that we couldn't see but actually showed up on what was called a BEAM MRI (a specific x-ray of the brain.) We were told he could not control what was going on in his head – similar to having hundreds of radios playing different stations in your head, all at once. There was no way for him to listen, understand or focus.

Surprisingly this latest disorder was relatively easy to treat, after a short three-month stint. At first, Aaron was placed on Tegretol, an anticonvulsant medication which made him vomit all the time. Then he was switched to Trileptal, which he took twice daily. Explosive combative behavior finally addressed. Check!

One of the MANY battles royal I had with Don, stemmed from Aaron's placement after each and every RTC confinement. You can't just send a kid home after he receives supervised treatment, specialized professional therapy, controlled meds and, most of all, the non-negotiable aspect – structure.

Treatment for these kinds of disorders is like a four-legged stool. These kids desperately need medication, consistent therapy, strong, united family support and a structured environment in which to return home. To say Aaron's environment at home was structured is like calling the sinking of the Titanic a small boating mishap.

With two parents arguing constantly about Aaron's much-needed treatment, you wouldn't know they were actually speaking of the same child! One parent thought Aaron was psycho and the other truly believed there was nothing wrong with him.

Really?

After Aaron's completion of the Meridell program, we faced the same ongoing battle – where does Aaron go now? Arizona Children's Association wouldn't take him back (what a surprise). Onward this time, to yet another treatment center in Scottsdale, Arizona. The staff was big and burley…a good sign.

I asked the director why there were three 8-hour shifts of caregivers at all the RTC's with which we had previously interacted. He pointed out how exhausting it was dealing with these children/young men day in and day out. He said sometimes even an 8-hour shift was too long!

I arranged for the president of the state Tourette Syndrome chapter to present what is called an 'in-service' to the RTC staff and I spoke briefly on what it meant to live with a son with so many issues. I took it upon myself to ask one of the caregivers if he thought our little presentation was helpful. His answer was, "I'd piss on a spark plug if I thought it would help me understand better!"

Chapter 11
Motor Home to Tucson

Around the year 1998, when Aaron was 12 years old, he was a regular patient of Dr Richard Popeski in Tucson, one of the Southwest's most well-respected and renowned psychiatrists specializing in the treatment of Tourette Syndrome.

Don bought a 34-foot motorhome so we could travel there for Aaron's appointments with a handy dandy bathroom in tow. The very first time we took it out, Don decided to grab some food at the local Burger King and accidentally tore out the entire overhang in the drive thru lane. Motor homes and drive thru fast food restaurants are not meant to be interactive!

We tried to sleep in the parking lot of the doctor's office but being in such close quarters with Aaron and his sister was not my idea of fun. We ended up driving that big boat to Tucson every other weekend and then getting a hotel room. Smart, seasoned travelers, we were not! We did this for four solid years – were we dedicated parents trying desperately to help our son or just a family of four delusional lunatics? You tell me.

At one point, I was pleading with Dr Popeski to make Don understand how unhappy and truly SCARED I was for Lauren's safety and mine. Aaron would give me detailed descriptions about how he was planning to go into Lauren's room and murder her. Then he was going to come into my room and murder me as well. His dad? Well, Aaron said he was going to let HIM live.

Typical exchange between us and still nothing new. I remember Dr Popeski asking Don if he was REALLY listening to my concerns about our safety. I was always complaining that Don was not listening to me, and Don argued that I was overreacting YET AGAIN. We seemed never to be able to get past that point.

Dr Popeski told us that he categorized his Tourette patients on a 1–15 scale with 15 being the worst with exaggerated tics and deficits. He told us unequivocally that Aaron was the worst '15' he had ever seen in his career.

What a GREAT claim to fame!!! And Don remained silent.

Chapter 12
Sony Game

Aaron was addicted to playing some Sony game that interacted with players all across the country and the world. He would have played it 24/7 if we let him. His actual physical confrontations and fights with people ALWAYS had to do with someone not letting him play this game on his computer.

There was the time that he pulled a butter knife from the kitchen drawer and was brandishing it at one of the caregivers at home. What was his reason for this felony action? Aaron wanted to play 'his game' and wasn't allowed to use the computer at that time because he had to do his homework, give fresh water to the dogs or complete some important chore.

Life with Aaron was NEVER dull. Something unbelievable was always happening. One time, we heard a knock on our front door one early Sunday morning. Don and I looked out the front window and saw it was two sheriff's deputies.

I stayed back while Don opened the door. All of a sudden, this horrific commotion ensued. The two deputies grabbed Don, threw him down on the floor and handcuffed him behind his back.

I was frantic trying to find out what had just happened and why!

Turns out Aaron was actually playing his game, Everquest, and had told the other players online that his father was beating him regularly, physically abusing him and starving him to death. Apparently, Sony actually monitors some of these games and reported Aaron's comments to the authorities. Because we lived out in the county, the sheriff's department was dispatched.

Luckily, there were no charges filed against Don. The deputies saw how well-fed Aaron was and couldn't find a single bruise on his body. As punishment, he was banned from playing Everquest for the rest of his life.

Another time, Aaron called Child Protective Services and actually told them we were starving him. He reported that he was so hungry he was trying to eat his own arm. When CPS showed up and took one look at Aaron, they realized this kid had NEVER missed a meal in his life! Like I said, there was never a dull moment living with Aaron.

Chapter 13
Sleepwalking

One of Aaron's many peculiarities was his sleepwalking through the house at night. We only discovered this when I realized someone had been peeing on the piano in the living room. The doctors thought this peculiarity was the side effect of one of the many different medications he was taking.

We had just built a swimming pool in the backyard because the kids were 11 and 9. They had been swimming for a number of years so I thought it finally would be safe to have one. This brought another set of challenges because I was afraid that despite the pool being fully fenced, Aaron's sleepwalking would lead him outside and land him in the water at night where he would drown.

After the swimming pool was completed, we then installed an elaborate alarm and fire system – NOT to keep burglars OUT but to ensure we kept Aaron IN!

I'm so glad we installed the smoke detector system at that time…One night, the alarms were going off like crazy and I dashed out of our upstairs bedroom around two in the morning. I ran smack into Aaron, who had come up from his downstairs bedroom to wake us.

In my sleepy haze, I asked Aaron what he had been doing since he clearly was not sleepwalking during this latest incident. He said he was hungry. I turned from the bedroom and dashed off to the kitchen which I found was clouded in smoke. I grabbed the fire extinguisher and ploughed my way to the microwave which was on fire and burning brightly.

Aaron had decided to make popcorn and had set the microwave for two hours instead of two minutes!

And Don slept through it all.

Chapter 14
Equine Therapy

At some point, Don and I decided to add equine therapy to our ever-growing bag of tricks.

According to my stepdaughter, Kristin Foree Tobias, horses have long been known to possess many attributes that may encourage healing in humans. Winston Churchill was quoted as having said, "There is nothing better for the inside of a man than the outside of a horse."

Equine Facilitated Therapy is used to treat many psychological and neurological disorders. Its benefits include exercise, confidence building, empathy training and recreation. This unique combination of factors makes it useful in treating traumatic brain injury, cerebral palsy, autism and mental illness, just to name a few. It is believed that the horse offers a non-judgmental relationship and can act as a therapeutic facilitator.

Equine therapy offers an opportunity for these kids to heal their hearts and find the tools to achieve personal goals in rather a most unlikely place – a barn. And, if there was anything that could perhaps help enhance Aaron's emotional, behavioral and cognitive skills – all we could say was, "Sign us up!"

Now being the calm, cool and collected parents that we were, did we bother looking into purchasing an old nag or a horse who had seen better days? Of course not. We ended up purchasing not one, but TWO, fancy, well-bred horses that not only came with great lineage but some pretty hefty price tags as well. Laura Jean (a distant relative of Secretariat) and April's Lark, joined the Engler household when the kids were about eight and ten. We were at least smart enough to stable them where people knew exactly what they were doing.

All I knew about horses at that time was that they all looked alike because each one had four legs and a tail.

After about a year, Aaron decided to give up his jockey days. Why, you might ask? Because he said the saddle was hurting his private parts. However, during those 12 months he learned more about horses than I'll ever learn in two lifetimes. I remember an incident where a new colt slipped through a gate and accidentally separated from its mother. Mom horse was trying to tear down her stall and the entire facility, trying to get to her baby.

My jaw dropped at what happened next. Aaron slowly approached the new baby and spoke to it in a soft, soothing voice. He gently wrapped his arms around the colt and carried it back into the stall with its mother. While watching all this, a feather could have knocked me over.

Did I mention, we ended up with 97 horses because Don purchased them all as pets? He told me he liked having coffee with them because they didn't talk back. Really?

The Gifted Horse program in Los Alamos, N.M.

Chapter 15
Volatility, Violence and Then Some!

In addition to Aaron's run in with Valley Horizon School and two separate brushes with the law, Aaron was accumulating a rather disturbing history of hurting people. Don's way of dealing with it only made it worse!!!

Aaron's best and only friend at the time was Edgar. Why he put up with Aaron, I'll never know. I would like to think he saw the good in Aaron and was able to overlook all the crazy stuff. But even Edgar had his limits. One time, he called the house to inform Don and me that Aaron pulled a knife on him. Instead of trying to understand the concern and fear that Edgar was conveying, Don attacked, "What did you do to him that made him so angry?"

"I wouldn't let him have a soda from the refrigerator because Mrs. Engler said not to."

Another time, Aaron was at a local park playing with some other kids. At one point, Aaron became furious with one of the other children and started choking him. Thank goodness, Edgar was there and wrestled Aaron off this poor kid who was literally turning blue. Aaron turned around and lunged at Edgar and took a HUGE (and I do mean BIG!) bite out of his stomach. You could actually see the teeth marks on his skin!

These were the types of issues I was dealing with on an everyday basis. To say it was stressful and exhausting is the understatement of the century. I don't know with whom I was most frustrated – Aaron, for making my life so difficult or Don, for turning a blind eye to it all.

Don was absent, both as a husband and father, so much so that my new girlfriend, Kathy, went MONTHS before she first met him. At one point, she took me aside and confided that she understood why I kept my husband 'under wraps'. She had seen our obese, unshaven, smelly handyman with no teeth at my house and calmly said she now knew why we were never seen together – SHE THOUGHT THE HANDYMAN WAS DON!

Chapter 16
What Challenges?

Let me give you a number of illustrations of a few of the issues with which I had to deal with my son.

The first is called sensory overload. This is a heightened awareness of touch and noise. A good analogy is wearing a mohair sweater over a third-degree sunburn. That's what sensory overload felt like to him. God forbid, I left any remnant of a tag on one of his shirts.

When Aaron was old enough to play soccer, every coach in Yuma wanted him on their team because of his size. Little did they know that while other kids were kicking the ball towards the goal, there sat Aaron, picking the grass in center field. He said there were too many kids running around at the same time and it upset him.

Whatever Aaron was experiencing was 'NORMAL' for him. Trying to control the never-ending movement of his different body parts, suppressing his tics, getting ridiculed and laughed at by his peers...non-stop! Then add in over-reactive discipline from his parents, and you have this utter exhaustion that is just a part OF his everyday existence.

My challenge, as his mom and fiercest advocate, was to figure out how to help him overcome all these problems and still evolve, with his self-esteem intact.

Addressing Aaron's hierarchy of ongoing problems was also a monumental task. Is it the tics that are making the kid (and teacher) crazy? Is it the hyperactivity? Which of the many problems do you need to address first? Which ones do you let slide?

Aaron's lack of social skills was as painful to me as it was for him. He so desperately wanted to belong, but didn't know how. He was so self-involved, just trying to survive! When he was under extreme stress, which was pretty constant, his frontal lobes just crashed. Then he couldn't process ANYTHING!

At times, Aaron's lights (the frontal lobes) would turn on, and he would do just great in school. But the next day, for whatever reason (the $64 million question!) the lights would turn off again. His teachers repeatedly asked me how my child did so well in school one day, and why he was such a terror the next. If either of us knew, we would certainly have revealed the big secret. But neither of us had a clue!

Aaron's teachers said what they needed from me were practical solutions for the various challenges they faced. For example, he would constantly tap his pencil in class. I came up with the idea of placing a mousepad on the desk under his pencil so no one could hear it. Also, when Aaron found himself in a particularly stressful situation that was escalating, I suggested his teachers send him out of the classroom with instructions to deliver an 'important' envelope to the attendance office. Nobody knew it was actually empty. Poor Aaron trudged many a mile delivering blank notes all over his school.

Aaron also had a severe case of coprolalia. This disorder is the involuntary utterance of offensive or obscene words and phrases, particularly the use of obscenities, racial slurs and sexually charged language. It differs from swearing or insulting others in that it is involuntary and extremely difficult for the person to control. It's like trying to suppress a sneeze...forever!

We learned to THINK OUT OF THE BOX every single day. We invented a new word together. Instead of 'mother f-bomb, the N word, shit' and other such special words, I came up with 'Farganizel', which Aaron FINALLY learned to blurt out instead.

It was painful for me to watch Aaron try so hard to hold in his tics. Kids with Tourette's can't concentrate on their classwork when all their energy and efforts are going full force somewhere else. These kids often put forth greater efforts in their schoolwork than their peers but with significantly less results.

I felt like I was sending Aaron out to war every single day. I had to let him loose to handle situations on his own in the cafeteria, the playground, the hallway – all of which were places in which he couldn't tolerate the over-stimulation. I desperately wanted him to be able to pat himself on the back simply for having made it through another school day.

Think of your most stressful day at work. We are talking the worst stressor you can imagine. (For me, it's getting off chocolate!) Take that tension, times it by 1000 and THAT'S what Aaron lived with, day in and day out!

Aaron also suffered from what I call 'The Black Hole Syndrome'. He had no executive function and couldn't organize anything. We used to have three sets of schoolbooks...one for him to lug around, one in each classroom for when he forgot (which was always!) and a third set at home for us to help him complete the work he had not finished in the classroom.

Then we had to deal with the non-verbal learning disability...the lack of processing in his brain. Aaron would read something, hear you explain it, and yet his brain couldn't process it. He could explain verbally what was in his head, but could not translate it to paper.

Written expression is so very difficult for these kids. Studies show that 90% of kids with Tourette Syndrome, Obsessive Compulsive Disorder, Attention Deficit Disorder, NEVER go on autopilot. They can't think about content AND handwriting at the same time. Needless to say, school was not Aaron's most favorite place in the world!

My most important strategy was to KEEP MY SENSE OF HUMOR. I just knew that God himself couldn't teach these kids!!! Remember that Tics R US! I also learned that these kids are usually 2/3 the chronological age in maturity and judgment i.e., when Aaron was 12 years old, he had the maturity and judgment of an 8-year-old.

When I would talk to Aaron, it was critical that I check for comprehension. I learned how important it was to pause frequently in between a sequence of instructions.

When I got angry with Aaron, I couldn't assume he knew why. I would slowly and carefully explain why I was upset and specifically tell him what he needed to do better the next time. I learned to avoid the word 'don't'.

When I would say, "Don't slam the door," all Aaron's brain processed was the part that said, "Slam the door." And that's exactly what he did. But I learned I had to replace the negative with a positive such as, "Close the door quietly." Instead of saying, "Don't touch the wall," I would say "Put your hands in your pocket." Whatever you do, "DON'T SAY DON'T!!!"

These kids need to be taught exactly what to do in every foreseeable situation…we, as parents, have to make sure they always have an answer. They freeze in new situations and are not able to generate a response on their own. It is critical that they learn how to conduct themselves in certain situations and practice it over and over and over again. For example, greeting the teacher: It took Aaron and me months to rehearse this and his teacher just about fell over the first time he said to her, "Good morning, Mrs. Klee."

I learned how important it was to always make sure Aaron had a plan…how shall we deal with this? Brainstorm and come up with a plan in advance such as, "When you go into the lunch room, you get your tray, sit down and finish your lunch before you get up to go outside to play." Very direct, specific directions, are what these kids need.

Many kids with neurological deficits respond to consequences…not punishment. They get a completely different message. They need continuous simple positive reinforcement and, it's more effective when it's ongoing. They are unable to organize their thoughts or feelings to learn from negative punishment. They will only focus on the punitive aspect of it and never learn from it. You need to look at what needs to be done for the child to PREVENT THE

BEHAVIOR instead of looking at what to do to the child AFTER the behavior occurs.

For four years in a row, Aaron ate the exact same lunch at school – two peanut butter sandwiches and a package of Fig Newtons. One day, he was supposed to go to an assembly and eat lunch at a different school. Aaron got so agitated over the upcoming change in his routine that I needed to figure out what to do to help him in this new scenario. So, I made prior arrangements with his teacher that he be allowed to bring his standard peanut butter sandwiches and Fig Newtons to the different school lunch. Problem solved.

We had a tradition in our house where we had pizza for dinner every Friday night. One day I dared to bring home pizza on a Wednesday night – Aaron became so upset about eating pizza on the wrong day that I saved his slice for him until Friday night.

Aaron once explained to me that holding in his tics was like trying to suppress a sneeze…you can only do it so long and it has to come out sometime. Some days, he was able to control his tics at school but that would put him into what he called 'overload'. Home was Aaron's sole safe haven. There, he could just let his tics explode. It broke my heart at times, seeing him desperately holding his breath to control his tics when they were really bad.

Chapter 17
Obsessive Compulsive Disorder (OCD) on Steroids

My most vivid recollection of Aaron's OCD on display was on my birthday, April 28, 1997. Aaron was ten years old and Lauren was eight.

Since it was supposed to be 'my day' I chose Mandarin Palace for an early dinner that night. The restaurant was situated next door to the Mandarin Movie Theater and my favorite disaster movie of all time, 'Volcano' starring Tommy Lee Jones, was playing at the most perfect time. My mind started to churn. We could watch the movie first, eat junk food at the show and then go to dinner afterwards.

What a BRAINSTORM!!!

I was practically hopping up and down with excitement!!! My idea of a great movie is watching a disaster unfold right in front of my eyes from the safety and security of either my television set or a movie screen. This birthday was going to be my 'Heaven on Earth!'

Ya think?

I told the kids that I REALLY, REALLY, REALLY wanted to see this movie then and there. Lauren was good with it. Aaron...not so much!

"Mom, it's Wednesday at 4 p.m. You know I only go see movies on Sunday at 12:18 p.m."

"If you make me go to the movie right now, I will probably have to miss school tomorrow. I won't be able to do any homework tonight because movies are not part of my Wednesday routine. Please don't make me go to the movies on a Wednesday!"

Well, Aaron was ramping it up to the next level and his pleas were getting louder and more pathetic. It was escalating beyond both his and my control. Enter Godzilla!

Don started in on Aaron with, "How selfish can you be? It's your mother's birthday and can't you just do the one thing she wants to do today – go see a movie?"

At that point Aaron repeated his multiple pleas and reasons for NOT going to a movie on Wednesday afternoon – only LOUDER and more frenzied!

After yelling at Aaron for being the most selfish kid on the planet, Don stalked away and went into the restaurant. I saw my request was a lost cause and slowly followed him in with both kids in tow. When we sat down, I tried to explain to Don that it was Aaron's OCD kicking into overdrive and why didn't he see that? Instead of yelling at Aaron and calling him selfish, I wanted Don to be more responsive to Aaron's angst.

Don's reaction to that suggestion was to storm out of the restaurant and drive home. Thank goodness we came in two cars. I was getting so used to being alone with the kids and having to light and blow out my own birthday candles…

Chapter 18
Three Times Is Not the Charm!

At the age of ten if I thought trying to get Aaron to watch a movie with me any day of the week except Sunday was a problem, his latest 'tic' of touching people on the shoulder three times was even more challenging.

I have to admit – there were times when Aaron was getting so worked up because he couldn't finish touching Lauren the second and third time that I actually considered just letting him do it!!! Having Lauren upset with me because Aaron was in her personal space was easier to handle than dealing with his outrageous uncontrolled outburst because he couldn't complete his third touch. What kind of miserable mother was I???

During this time, Aaron tried hard but could not control himself in public. He would walk up to total strangers and touch them on the shoulder three times. Short of keeping him isolated at the house except for school, I was at my wit's end trying to substitute this tic for something more socially acceptable.

At one point, he turned his attention to the car radio and blasted the volume up not once, not twice but...you got it – THREE times! And God help anyone who tried to keep him from completing that third touch!

I honestly expected Aaron's special education counselor at school to understand his latest and greatest three-touch tic. She, of all the people in the world, SHOULD HAVE KNOWN BETTER than report to the local police that his latest and greatest tic had sexual connotations. This was just one of the many surprises we had coming our way…

Aaron and Lauren

Chapter 19
Are We Having Fun Yet?

Living with Aaron was a challenge each and every single day. I was tasked with teaching him the basics of life – such as how to take a shower.

Aaron strolled out of the bathroom and I asked him – did you wash your hair? He said no. Did you wash your private parts? He said no. Did you use any soap? He said no.

"What the heck were you doing in there?" I asked him. He answered in a dead serious tone – "I took a shower like you told me to."

That's the moment I learned how to make the laminating machine my new best friend. I printed out a list of items he needed to pay attention to in the shower and laminated it to make it waterproof. Then I hung it on the showerhead so he could use it as a checklist for all future showers.

Kids like Aaron need LOTS of extra prodding for their brains to process what 'normal' kids' brains can do automatically. Experts cite that a 'special needs' brain needs 40 imprints on it, in order for it to finally make an impact and be retained.

My motto was, 'Tell him, tell him again and then tell him again what you just told him.' Eventually it MIGHT sink in!!!

Being Aaron's mom was all about the necessary creativity that came from living with a child with special needs.

I remember when we moved into my dream house in town in 2001. I spent three years building it and was wildly excited when it was finally time to move in. Living in the outskirts, where no one would deliver pizza, was becoming problematic for me. This new house was smack in the middle of town and Pizza Hut was finally able to find me!

But there were some downsides, too. For instance, moving from a 6000 square foot home into a smaller one was extremely stressful. But when you throw Aaron into the mix, you're setting yourself up for a nervous breakdown!

Lauren jumped right in and unpacked her room the first time she was asked. But Aaron...not so much.

I told him, no less than a dozen times, that he needed to be the one to sort through the boxes and put his personal belongings away. One evening I also asked him to bring me an onion from the garage, which he did, while I was preparing one of our very first dinners in our new house.

Later, I just lost it and started screaming at Aaron, threatening that if he didn't unpack his stuff, I was just going to burn it all. He just looked at me with this innocent, uncomprehending gaze and said, "I brought you your onion – wasn't that good enough?"

After bursting into tears from both frustration and pain, I remembered that Aaron's frontal lobes had not turned on yet – the lights were on but there was no one home. My dad used to say that Aaron had "scrambled eggs for brains".

Chapter 20
Dr. Morton Doran

About this time in our lives, enter Dr. Morton Doran, a successful neurosurgeon with what he calls 'full-blown' Tourette's. He has vocal tics and a compulsion to tap people and items with his hands. At times his hands have a mind of their own, jerking uncontrollably in uncoordinated movements. He confesses that, in public, he must control those actions because it is not socially acceptable to touch people we do not know.

Without his medication, he is spastic. However, in the operating room, his hands are perfectly steady, and his mind remains laser focused. Many news articles have been written about him. The world-renowned writer and neurologist, Oliver Sacks, wrote a short story that appeared in The New Yorker Magazine on March 16, 1992 about a surgeon with Tourette's, based on the life of Dr. Doran.

That lengthy article detailed what it was like for this doctor to see patients, perform surgeries AND fly his own private airplane. Dr. Doran laughingly claimed he was the world's only pilot with Tourette's.

I learned through my state TS chapter that Dr. Doran wintered in Tucson, Arizona and enjoyed speaking to Tourette's support groups throughout the state. Well, if he enjoyed it, I was going to make sure he enjoyed it in Yuma.

When he first flew to Yuma from Tucson in his private airplane and I picked him up, I was taken aback by his constant involuntary body movements. How does one fly an airplane when they are ticking all over the cockpit? "Very carefully," he responded.

During his presentation to the Yuma TS chapter, Dr. Doran explained how a person with TS can challenge himself to succeed. At age 60, he finally acknowledged being able to limit many of his tics and other odd behaviors when he's in public.

"If a person uses a wheelchair because he has spinal cord damage, people understand. But if the wiring problem is in the brain, the public fails to recognize that the visible signs – such as shouting obscenities – are the result of a physical ailment."

"These kids can do everything. Accept what you can't change, change what you can and get on with living," Doran told his audience. "Give the child confidence to say, 'I'm going to do it, despite my Tourette Syndrome.'"

Dr. Doran's presentation to the Yuma support group was extremely well received. Did my son even bother to meet this incredible person who could have been such an important role model in his life? Of course not!

His dad said he did not want Aaron to hang around other people who might have been considered crazy.

"I'm going to do it"

Doctor presents his experiences living with Tourette's syndrome

By MICHELE COHEN
Yuma Daily Sun Staff Writer

Mort Doran's hand trembles briefly as he talks. He repeatedly picks at the shoulders of his polo shirt and touches the top of his mustache. If he were a child, you might say he fidgeted.

At age 60, He has learned to limit many of his tics and other odd behaviors when he is in public.

Doran demonstrates how a person with Tourette's syndrome can challenge himself to succeed. A surgeon, he practices during the summer in Cranbrook, British Columbia, and winters in Tucson, where he lectures in anatomy at the University of Arizona Health Science Center.

If a person uses a wheelchair because he has spinal cord damage, people could understand, Doran told a Yuma audience recently. But if the wiring problem is in the brain, the public fails to recognize the visible signs — such as shouting obscenities — are the result of a physical ailment.

Tourette's syndrome is a "medical neurobiological condition as real as heart disease," that shows itself as tics and behavioral problems. Tics are repeated involuntary movements of any part of the body. Sometimes, the muscles involved cause vocalizations, such as barking, throat clearing or sniffing, although they are really no different than the silent tics of his shaking arm.

About two-thirds of people with Tourette also have obsessions and compulsions and/or are hyperactive and impulsive. Doran said his case would be considered more severe than many, since he has all the symptoms. French physician Georges Gilles de la Tourette first described the condition in 1884.

Doran didn't discover that his behavior matched those of the syndrome until he was 37 because it is so rare.

The National Institute of Health estimates that 100,00 Americans have full blown TS, according to the National Tourette Association. Some genetic studies suggest that the figure may be as high as one in 200f those with chronic multiple tics and/or transient childhood tics are included in the count.

Doran describes his movements as a sort of super-sensitivity to external cues. Just as a person might be bothered by a clothing tag on a collar, Doran senses something isn't quite right like a 1,000 tags tugging all over his body.

"It's like a psychic itch you have to scratch," Doran said. The current theory about the cause of Tourette is rooted in the evolution of the brain and involves abnormal

Dr. Morton Doran, surgeon and educator at the University of Calgary medical school.

The current theory about the cause of Tourette is rooted in the evolution of the brain and involves abnormal metabolism of several brain chemicals called neurotransmitters. The outer cortex is the thinking, dreaming, planning portion that controls judgement and impulses. The paleocortex is the older, more primitive instinctive area that is inhibited by the outer cortex in modern human beings.

In TS, instinctive gut reactions emerge that seem irrational to others.

"It's a defensive mechanism," he explained.

When Tourette occurs, the connections between the portions appear to develop imperfectly early in fetal development or in early childhood, according to research. There is believed to be a genetic factor , but environment may play a role, Doran said. Other evidence suggests a link between infection of a particular strain of strep bacteria and the appearance of TS symptoms.

About 20% of 5 to 7-year-olds develop tics that leave as suddenly as they appear, Doran said. The end of the tics may be a result of the maturation of brain circuits that fails to happen in TS.

Today, he can hold back his response to similar patterns long enough to get out of earshot.

The hallmark of TS is a lack of inhibition so that all thoughts, actions and emotions are released. In Doran's case, he would skip through the hallways of the hospital when no one was looking. But not all of Doran's symptoms are so benign. He has been prone to rages, tossing whatever was at hand.

Doran has learned over time to recognize the triggers that set him off. The sounds Doran's father made when he ate made it impossible for him to be in the room without an outburst.

Today, he can hold back his response to similar patterns long enough to get out of earshot.

"The question is not how to control the rage, but to prevent it or modify it," he said.

Drugs to stimulate or suppress chemical reactions in the brain may be used if a group of symptoms significantly interferes with daily living. For example, Doran takes medication that reduces his obsessional behavior, which was wasting huge amounts of his day.

Doran suggests a child with Tourette's syndrome must learn that there are consequences for poor behavior and the family and others must work with the child to set limits on what will be tolerated.

"You can't let them get away with everything. They have to take responsibility for some things," he said.

He also offers hope to families coping with Tourette's syndrome.

"These kids can do everything. Accept what you can't change, change what you can and get on with living," Doran said.

"Give the child confidence to say, 'I'm going to do it despite my Tourette's syndrome.' "

Chapter 21
Advocating for Special Needs Children

Thanks to all my on-going trials and tribulations living with Aaron, I was becoming the 'Go-To Mom' for helping other frazzled mothers. My daughter was 16-years-old at the time and introduced her manager to me, from the Subway sandwich shop, where she was working. She told her boss, "You need to really speak to my mom. She can help anyone!"

I immediately met her and her seven-year-old son at my office and jumped right in with both feet!

The poor woman was a single mom and her son was non-verbal and profoundly autistic. He had never attended public school and was being home schooled by his grandmother, who recently died. The boy did not know how to go to the bathroom or even dress himself.

Additionally, the mom was having to walk to work every day because she did not even own an automobile.

Carol to the rescue!

The first thing I did was purchase an inexpensive car for her to take her son to the Yuma office of the Department of Developmental Disabilities (DDD) to sign him up for services. Piece of cake!

Wrong!!!

The boy had never been to a doctor and had not received any childhood vaccinations. Because he had never seen a doctor, there was no written diagnosis or records of any kind. So, I personally paid for him to be seen by a local doctor and get whatever DDD deemed necessary to get him into 'the system'. Easy enough, right?

Wrong again!

Every time I went back to this agency to see when the young man could begin his desperately needed services, there were new and additional stumbling blocks thrown in our way. After about the fifth trip and being rejected one more time, I lost it.

I happened to be driving to Phoenix that day for another meeting. I calmly told the caseworker I was so done with her and that I needed the name of her supervisor...NOW! I was going to meet with him or her in person and have them explain to my face why this child could not get DDD services.

Before I drove out of the Yuma DDD parking lot, I received a call on my cell phone...congratulating me on the fact that this boy was miraculously approved for services, right then and there. What a coincidence!

His services began and to be honest, I became so busy helping other parents with their special needs kids that I'm embarrassed to admit that I stopped following up with what I called 'The Subway Mom'.

To my utter surprise and delight, about five years later, she surprised me and suddenly showed up at my office one day. Not only did she pay me back for the cost of the car I bought for her, but the most amazing event that was off the Richter Scale happened right then in front of my eyes.

Her son walked up to me, put out his hand and said, "Thank you!" This, from a kid who, five years earlier, was non-verbal and not even toilet trained!

I burst out crying with joy and gave them both the biggest bear hug I could muster through my non-stop flow of happy tears.

If God is keeping score, then I definitely got an 'A' on my heavenly report card for this one!

Another standout advocacy story occurred on Christmas Eve. I received a frantic call from a mother whose nine-year-old son, I will call Johnny, was being arrested by the police for his volatile behavior at home. I had been advocating for him at school and helping his mother understand that he wasn't really a 'bad' kid. He was suffering from multiple undiagnosed mental health issues, which she did not have the first clue how to handle.

I rushed down to find several Yuma police cars in front of their house. I heard a lot of yelling and angry shouting inside. When I finally worked my way through the front door, I explained to the police that this young boy was not a juvenile delinquent but actually needed some immediate mental health assistance.

After talking to multiple police officers until I was blue in the face, I was finally able to convince them that they should take the child to the local hospital for a psychiatric evaluation – NOT the Yuma County juvenile detention center.

Eventually, we all ended up in a special room in the emergency department where I spent several hours with the mom, child and only ONE police officer, reassuring him repeatedly that the child had some serious emotional issues and needed to be treated professionally – not jailed. Detention was not even remotely an option in my mind.

I ended up flying Johnny and his mother to the same Meridell Achievement Center in Austin, Texas, that Aaron had attended. Johnny, too, was diagnosed with Complex Seizure Disorder. Once he left that psychiatric facility with the proper combination of medications, he went on to become an excellent student, graduating from the local school system, without further incident.

Chalk up another good grade on that report card in heaven!

I am one of the few remaining old-fashioned creatures who still read the actual local newspaper every single morning. Touching actual hard copy vs. the internet, has been my routine for the past 40-plus years and I have NO intention of changing it now.

One morning, I read on the front page that an elementary school boy with Tourette Syndrome had been arrested and charged with assault because he 'slapped' his teacher's hand. REALLY???

Yuma being the small town it was (and still is), I was able to identify and locate the mom and child to see if I could be of some assistance. Yes, they gratefully replied. They needed all the help they could get!

Apparently going multiple times to the boys' restroom was an ongoing 'issue' with this young child, whom I recall was in the third grade. The teacher apparently refused to let the kid go, grabbed his wrist and would not let him go, even though his government mandated Individualized Education Plan (IEP) specifically stated he would be allowed to go as often as needed.

It seems the incident escalated when the boy suddenly slapped his teacher's hand in an attempt to escape the death grip on his wrist. And that's when the war began.

The principal of the school joined the melee, called the police, and had the child arrested, charging him with assault on the teacher. No overreaction on her part.

Having been an investigative reporter for the local newspaper in a previous life, I set about discovering all the facts of 'The Crime'. It turns out the district's head of special education, my good friend Sal, was out of town at a conference when this incident came down.

When I called him to offer my help, we spoke frankly about the overreaction of the teacher AND the principal. It also didn't hurt 'our' case that my son's amazing criminal attorney had offered to represent this child pro bono (for free).

Sal and I set up a meeting with everyone involved in 'The Crime' – and I mean EVERYONE. We had the mom and son, the teacher, the principal, some of the classroom kids as witnesses, the police officer, Sal, the school's attorney – I think even the janitor attended!

Long story short – the school district apologized to the family, dropped the criminal charges against the child and agreed to let him attend any school the family chose. The district also threw in bus transportation if the newly selected school happened to be out of the child's home boundaries.

Score another one for the special needs kiddo! I should be batting 1000 in Heaven!

Unfortunately, not all of my advocacy stories had a happy ending. And I had no one to blame but myself.

Chapter 22
The Pumphouse

I really can't say I ever knew what I was thinking when I was constantly trying to 'save the whole world'. Maybe by helping all these other kids I would be helping Aaron in some convoluted way. I, still to this date, do not understand my burning desire to help everyone that came into my life.

A dear friend of mine married a man who had experience in running a group home for young men with special needs, addictions, issues, etc. He professed to be the alternative for juvenile detention and, unfortunately, I believed him lock, stock and barrel. He certainly talked the talk and knew all the right buzzwords.

My first clue should have been the difficulty he had in acquiring the necessary license to open such a facility in Yuma. The Arizona Department of Behavioral Health Services (BHS) was giving him the run around.

So, what did Carol do? What Carol does best – INTERFERE!!!

I drove up to Phoenix, sat at the BHS department's doorstep and negotiated back and forth between their case manager and the head of this boys' group home. Many faxes and signed documents later, I drove home with the newly issued group home state license in hand!

I had arranged for the group home to run out of my former residence, locally known as The Pumphouse. This important piece of Yuma history was built in 1921 by the United States Reclamation Service originally as the only way to irrigate the south Yuma Mesa. The property sits on the bank of the East-

Main Canal where it pulled the water and shot it up to the Mesa farmlands above.

It was one of the most impressive technological achievements of its time. Its grand opening drew the governors of Arizona, California and Sonora Mexico to celebrate the first use of Alternate Current (AC) electric motors to do the job that for generations had been performed by steam engines. It was a sign that Westinghouse/Tesla was winning the ongoing battle with Edison over how electricity was to be delivered.

In the mid-1950s, Yuma County farmers came up with concrete canals that became the norm for flood irrigation. This new form of watering became all the rage and The Pumphouse eventually sat abandoned for some 30-plus years.

In the 1970s, one of our local real estate developers thought it would make a great restaurant and began the task of converting the 6000 square foot dwelling into a viable business. The Pumphouse Restaurant opened for business in 1977 and I was one of the lucky invited guests! It became Yuma's premier location for fine dining. In fact, it was here that Don proposed marriage to me in 1978.

The Pumphouse

Rumor has it, The Pumphouse Restaurant was resold to a Yuma entrepreneur in the early 1980s. Unfortunately, before it shuttered its doors after a relatively short run, there were tales of rampant money laundering.

Public records showed no less than 14 liens, what we in real estate call 'clouds', on the title report including, but not limited to, the IRS, DES, the Arizona Department of Revenue, the Small Business Administration (SBA), unpaid property tax liens, judgments from the new owner's three ex-wives, The Pope – you name it, it was probably clouding this title.

So, when Don asked me to look into purchasing The Pumphouse for our future home, I thought he was nucking futz! I called the owner who told me, yes, he would love to sell to us, but the SBA won't agree. Then I called the SBA who said yes, they would love to sell to us, but the owner wouldn't agree. So, I went back to Don and told him it could not be bought. I sure as hell did not want to live out there in the boonies!

But, if the answer is no, then you're just not talking to the right person. Don promptly got on the phone and negotiated with the owner and the SBA. The Pumphouse was sold to Don and Carol Engler in 1984 for $80,000. Then came the fun and games of getting all 14 liens voluntarily lifted.

Much to Don's credit, he did know his law. He took hundreds of pictures of this abandoned, broken down structure and mailed them to everyone who had any kind of interest on the title. All agreed to voluntarily release their liens because they could clearly see there was no value to this property…that is, no value to anyone but Don.

Then came the remodel of the century which took an entire year and $50,000. That was a lot of money back in 1984. I could hardly sleep at night worrying about the $800 new monthly mortgage payment.

We moved into one of our rental homes for a year during this massive remodel. To put it mildly, it was not one of our better rental homes. "You mean other people pay us to live here?" Don asked.

We had three bachelor Marines as renters who apparently never cleaned the shower the entire year they lived there. "Did you ever clean the shower at least once?" I asked one of them. His stellar response was, "No, because every time we took a shower it got soapy and cleaned itself." Really?

This fortress known as The Pumphouse was constructed of 26-inch-thick poured concrete with rebar. When Yuma experienced small earthquakes, we felt nothing at our house for the first 18 years we lived there. Little did I know how fortunate I was to have such thick walls that were able to withstand a major house fire, even with the $40,000 fire suppression system I installed for the group home.

Chapter 23
Pumphouse Fire

Back to the 'infamous' group home which opened in 2003. At that time, I was on the board of the Arizona chapter of the National Tourette Syndrome Association. We regularly received requests from across the country for placement of troubled boys who had nowhere else to go for treatment.

For instance, I was contacted by the New York TSA chapter asking if I could help place a 13-year old boy I will call Sam. It appears, Sam was headed to juvenile detention if we could not find him a suitable living arrangement.

I told the New York chapter representatives and Sam's parents all about The Pumphouse and its ongoing program as a group home for young boys just like Sam. Before I could say 'Tourette Syndrome', Sam was delivered to Yuma and entered the program.

About a month after his arrival, a fire broke out in the three acres of scrub brush that surrounded the building. It burned the greenhouse next to the house and the Arizona Public Service power pole as well. Both nearby county access roads had to be closed because the brush was burning right up against the highway in all directions.

I received a call from the Rural Metro fire department telling me about the fire, so I dashed out there like the crazy lady I was. The front entrance road was blocked but I knew how to access my house from the canal below. I finally joined the crowd that had assembled in the parking lot of the home.

I must say, I was pretty darned impressed with how well the Rural Metro fire department kept the flames from overtaking my home. The surrounding area looked like my troubles, but the actual house was intact. YEA for our side!

It was later determined that Sam was the one who went outside and deliberately started the fire. Needless to say, his days at the Yuma group home came to an abrupt end and he was sent back home to his family.

Fast forward to July 2005 – right in the middle of my campaign for Mayor of Yuma, I got a call from the head of the group home telling me the boys were moving out of The Pumphouse permanently. I politely asked why there would be no notice…he replied, "Because of the fire." I asked, "What fire?"

Round two!!!

Allegedly, the fire suppression system had sprung a small leak the week before. Instead of telling me it needed to be repaired, the rocket scientist group home leader DISCONNECTED THE ENTIRE SPRINKLER SYSTEM!!! So, when a fire started downstairs in the basement for some unknown reason, it quickly spread throughout all the bedroom areas. No one was injured, thank God, but the entire downstairs was destroyed.

There is no way to describe the 'punch to the gut' feeling you get when you face the remnants of a house fire. I was speechless (definitely a first). My heart broke at the sight of my exercise equipment melted into one big blob. The concrete walls did not burn but the drywall did. Everything that did not burn was covered with black soot. Looking at my formerly beautiful Saltillo tile that was now totally black just added to my heartache and grief.

It took me more than a year to rebuild the downstairs of The Pumphouse. And to this day, I still don't believe the 'coincidence' that the fire suppression system was turned off just a few short days before the fire erupted. But that's another story.

Pumphouse fire

Chapter 24
Lauren's Physical Abuse

My mother had passed away December 31, 2001. My father was devastated and deep in the bowels of an understandably profound depression. My older sister, and my twin, and I decided to take him to Alaska on a cruise for his birthday to help lift his spirits.

I arranged for our nanny to take both Aaron and Lauren to Monterey, Mexico while I was gone to Alaska. The nanny had family there in Monterey and I was excited for them to experience a different culture. Don stopped traveling a long time ago, so he simply stayed home.

I remember getting an e-mail from Lauren telling me she had been rushed to a hospital in Mexico because Aaron had beaten up her face pretty badly. The picture she sent me showed a busted lip and two black eyes. I was frantic and literally wanted to swim back to the states to see with my own eyes if my daughter was all right.

As soon as I returned home, events continued to darken on the Engler marital horizon. I started looking into residential treatment center placement for Aaron yet again. I was not going to subject my daughter or myself to his explosive behavior any longer. Fifteen long years of this was more than enough.

My dear friend, Suzanne, just happened to be at our house at that moment and heard the explosive argument between Don and me. She practically cowered in the bathroom while Don had the audacity to ask Lauren what she did that made Aaron beat her up the way he did. Lauren told him she simply refused to give the laptop computer to Aaron when it was still her turn to play on it.

Who the hell blames the victim for being physically abused?

I was done. If you leave out the expletives, I had nothing to say. I basically told Don there was nothing he could ever say to me that would make me change my mind. It was definitely the beginning of the end for us. After only living in my 'forever' home for a whopping 14 months the end was here. I had my last and final fight with Don on a Thursday morning, and, by that Saturday afternoon, I had kicked both Aaron and him out of that beautiful gorgeous house. I bought and furnished a mobile home for them on the 20-acre horse ranch we owned and moved their booties there in record time. I had had enough!

After the two of them left (permanently) and were settled in their new digs, Lauren and I continued our lives as if nothing had happened.

Knowing that all my time and efforts had been focused on Aaron, I felt I definitely owed Lauren some 'mom and me' time. Jewish guilt is such a wonderful thing – I asked her what she felt would help her 'feel better' to make up for those lost years.

She told me a credit card and a dog – DONE! That was easy!!! She got an American Express card at the age of 16 and an adorable mutt named Hershey.

Eventually, I had to take away her credit card because she was putting gas in her friends' vehicles using the credit card that I was paying. They in turn gave her cash for the fuel. She made out like a bandit and I had never seen such ridiculously high gas bills! When I took the card away she told all her friends she was now destitute! But I still give her an 'E' for her entrepreneurial creativity!

The dog was another story…

Hershey was such a prima donna – she would not go to the bathroom outside if it had rained or the sprinklers had come on. While Lauren was sound asleep at 6 a.m., guess who

was running around the back yard with the dog in her arms –
looking for a dry spot for Her Highness to pee?

Chapter 25
What Was I Thinking???

At some crazy point, I had decided to run for Mayor of Yuma.
I was asked to consider this from the previous female mayor
whom I greatly admired. Sure, I can do this – piece of cake!

Despite working harder at this than anything else I had
ever done in my life, I lost the election miserably. No one in
Yuma wanted a female Jewish mayor! Some loser actually
spray-painted swastikas on my campaign signs!

My concession speech was simple and to the point – it's
not whether you win or lose at anything you attempt. It's how
well you played the game! Luckily, I lost the battle but
actually won the war!!!

After the election, I started dating Michael Foree, my
former campaign manager. At this point, Don and I had lived
apart for more than seven years, but I was legally still a
married woman. The only lie I ever told Mike was that I was
divorced when I really wasn't, because I knew he wouldn't
date me. I fessed up later in our relationship, after which he
had to endure my five-year divorce proceeding.

My now loving husband, was soooooo blonde back then
– I sent him not one, not two, but three thank you cards telling
him how much I appreciated his working on my campaign. I
also pointedly said in all three notes that if he ever wanted to
go out and have coffee or see a movie together, it would be
more fun than going it alone.

Absolutely no response – at all!!!

A few months later, I was at a local political function and
sitting alone at the bar. Someone came up to me and put his
hand on my shoulder, asking if he could buy me a drink.

I turned to look at Mike and distinctly said, "It's about time!"

A couple of drinks later, we decided to leave the function and go somewhere else for drinks. We closed up that bar and I pretended to be drunk. I asked Mike to drive me home. He pretended to be sober and did! The rest was history. We never looked back and I proceeded to go through with the actual divorce.

What was amazing to me was that even though Don and I had not lived together for seven years, both Aaron and Lauren were totally shocked and extremely upset that we were finally ending our 30-year marriage. I was baffled that they couldn't understand how miserable I was.

Lauren was around 17 years old at the time and particularly angry with me for dating Mike. One day he knocked on our front door and Lauren wouldn't even let him in. She shouted at him through the door that, "You're not half the man my father is!"

I ran to the front door to let Mike inside and promptly burst into tears. I asked him to say something profound (so I would stop crying). He looked me in the eye and said, "Shit happens!" He said that after teaching junior high students for some 32 years, that kind of stuff didn't bother him at all. When I finally stopped crying, I decided, come hell or high water, I was going to warm Lauren up to the idea that Mike and I were going to be together, hopefully for a very long time.

BAD IDEA!!!

Between Lauren's angst and raging hormones, she took it upon herself to move into her father's mobile home because I was the absolute worst mother in the entire universe. Why she moved BACK in the same house with Aaron, I will never understand. But how many 17-year-olds EVER make ANY sense?

Looking back, I spent the early part of Lauren's life valiantly trying to keep her safe from her explosive brother's violent outbursts. They went to separate schools, had separate friends and Aaron was in and out of one residential treatment center after another. We could never take him on a vacation with us and our two children basically lead totally separate lives.

One time, I did take both kids to McDonalds to burn off some energy in the ball pits. Aaron and another girl accidently bumped heads in that playhouse and I saw him rear back with his hand in a menacing fist as if to pummel the girl and I literally pole-vaulted into the ball pit. I grabbed Aaron and threw him off the girl he was about to punch. I don't think my feet ever touched the ground!

That was my last outing in memory where I took Aaron anywhere with me alone.

Prom night for Aaron and Lauren

Chapter 26
Mom to the Rescue!

Let's take a moment and go back to the dog – Lauren took Hershey during her move to the horse ranch. And Aaron and Hershey did not get along.

Previously, Aaron had broken the necks of five baby guinea pigs 'because he felt like it'. I was mortified when I took one of those poor little bodies to the vet for an autopsy…at which time I learned what actually killed them.

Aaron had also tried to drown Lauren's rabbit in the toilet. He also told me about a cat he had set on fire and that he was wanting to spew gasoline at a station and light a match to it.

So, when Aaron said he was going to kill Hershey – I had no doubt in my mind that he meant what he said. Mom to the rescue!

I grabbed a 75-year-old, dog-loving friend of mine, and we hurried over to Don's mobile home when we knew no one was there. We burst in, bundled up the dog and ran out like the two thieves we were! We burned rubber like there was no tomorrow and hauled our buns out of that ranch. I had actually never seen my elderly friend EVER move so fast!

My heart was breaking when Lauren was told that Hershey had run away. I couldn't bring myself to tell her the truth because I knew it would push her away even further.

But being silent didn't help. Lauren and I did not see each other or speak one word to each other for the first three years after I started dating Mike. She told me in no uncertain terms that I was NOT welcome at her high school graduation and that I had better not even THINK about attending.

Gee – I wasn't going to be able to sit in the stands in the Yuma heat for three whole hours watching thousands of kids parade across a stage. It was a tough job, but I was certain that I could rise to the task! I told everyone in my world that it was the quietest and best time of my life when in reality I was positively heartbroken. I had lost both my children to their dad.

Ironically, when Lauren and I finally made up in 2009, she told me how hurt and angry she was that I didn't attend her high school graduation!

Teenagers are the reason animals eat their young!!!

Chapter 27
Is It Divorce Time?

After Lauren moved out and left me all alone, Mike finally moved in and helped me prepare for the fight of my life – my pending divorce from Godzilla!

My attorney was from Tucson and told me I was her best frequent flyer. My divorce took five years from start to finish so you do the math. In the end, I thought it would have been cheaper to have put a bounty on Don's head and find a murder for hire kind of guy.

Don was representing himself in our divorce. The old adage 'an attorney who represents himself has a fool for a client' worked in his favor in this case. Every time the judge would rule against him he would appeal the decision. Each appeal cost me dearly. It didn't take too long, considering the cost of each appeal, to see that they were not going to be my friend!

I just loved Kathleen McCarthy, my attorney from Tucson – she was this feisty little gal who didn't take any of Don's crap. At one point during our depositions she asked him if she could call him Don. He said no, he would be Mr. Engler to her. She didn't skip a beat when she told him that from now on, I would be Ms. Engler to him!

One of the most ridiculous aspects of our divorce was Don's repeated requests for spousal maintenance and child support. What was he thinking? Aaron was 19 at the time and Lauren had been living with me.

The judge did chuckle and said something to the effect that the last time he looked at our case, Don was a working attorney and maybe he should work a little harder instead of looking to me for money.

My attorney told me to keep track of the money I was spending on both Aaron and Lauren (school supplies, prom clothing and expenses, food, etc.) so I could prove to the court that I was already carrying my end of the load. So, like an idiot, I tasked one of my secretaries to keep track of these bills so I could do what I do best – sell real estate.

Bad decision!

The secretary was working on this list when Lauren popped into my office and started reading it. Instead of asking ME what it was, she took 'Da List' to her dad and asked him what it was for. He wickedly told her I was keeping track of how much I was spending on Lauren because I was going to make her pay that money back!

It took YEARS for her to understand that her dad had flat out lied to her. It had nothing to do with any kind of payback. It was strictly for my attorney and the court. (To this day, I still don't think Lauren believes me!)

At one point, during our five-year Battle of the Roses, we had 97 horses at our horse ranch (which I named Whispering Horse Ranch after having seen Robert Redford's delectable backside in the movie Horse Whisperer.)

In my humble opinion, Don spent more time arguing with me about the value and outcome of the damn horses, than the future and security of his own children. Suddenly, all our real estate holdings that were going to me were worth millions of dollars but the horse ranch and all its occupants that he was getting were worthless. Really?

Chapter 28
Heart Surgery

Right in the middle of all this fighting, Don decided it was the perfect time to get ill and require an immediate five-way heart bypass surgery. Talk about added chaos to an already feuding family...I guess all those years of smoking three packs of cigarettes a day and a regular diet of fast food burgers and Mexican food took its toll on his ticker.

This was the second time Lauren had to bite the bullet and call me to tell me someone was ill. Apparently, her father wanted me to know what was happening so I could be some kind of comfort to our children in case his surgery went south (either that or he wanted to torture me some more because Lauren was still giving me the cold shoulder and acting as if her boyfriend's family members were the greatest thing since sliced bread.)

So, I sat there at the hospital, all by myself, for six-plus hours with no one to lean on or talk to (Aaron was mad at me again, for who knows what this time. I couldn't keep track.) But if Don wanted me there, I was going to do it despite feeling like an unwanted pariah the entire time.

When the surgeon came to speak to us, I jumped in as Don's current wife (soon to be ex was none of his business.) Lauren and I had a standoff right then and there, because she was the 17-year-old daughter and I was the monster who was divorcing her father...therefore, I should have had no standing in this drama.

During one of our many heated discussions, I asked Lauren why she didn't want me to be happy. I pointed out to her how miserable I was being married to her father, and that

I deserved to be happy. Her answer to me was that I promised to stay married to her father for better or worse, until death do us part. My snide comment back to her was that he didn't die so divorce was the next best thing.

A day or two later, I went to visit Don and bring some flowers. Lauren would not even let me come in his hospital room. It wasn't until Don told her it was OK to let me in that she reluctantly stepped aside. What did she think I was going to do to him – bring him a double cheese bacon burger with French fries from some fast food joint?

Speaking of fast food, when Don was released from the hospital the first thing he did was smoke a cigarette and then have Aaron take him to buy his first post-operative giant burger. Aaron was so torn because he knew Don was no longer supposed to smoke or eat these burgers on a regular basis. But alas, he did as his dad asked...always!

This brings to mind a time when Aaron was thoughtful enough to bring me a hamburger from some place...in the middle of the Yuma summer when it was close to 110 degrees. Not a problem in my mind because I had just paid the car mechanic to fix the air conditioning in the vehicle he drove.

With Aaron's frontal lobes still not turned on, he drove all the way to my house WITHOUT air conditioning because he didn't want MY hamburger to get cold. It was so dang hot outside he could have driven all the way to Phoenix with that same hamburger and it STILL would have remained warm!

By the time Aaron got to the house, he was a dehydrated dripping mess. I tried to explain to him that air conditioning was invented to be used – not turned off on days like this one, WITH OR WITHOUT A HAMBURGER!!!

Back to the second time Lauren was forced to speak to me. I remember getting a phone call at 4 a.m. and trying to decipher who was on the phone and why they were calling me at this ungodly hour.

Lauren was brusque, of course. I remember her saying Aaron had just been in a bad motorcycle accident and that her dad said I needed to come to the hospital immediately. Then she simply hung up.

Let me tell you all about Aaron and his multiple vehicles (as in more than one). As Aaron's mom, I didn't even want him to get a learner's permit, much less a driver's license.

The first week he was driving, he took our big Ford Bronco to school to pick up Lauren (unbeknownst to me). He gunned it through the parking lot and literally drove over some poor woman driving a Volkswagen. I was hysterical that my daughter was in a vehicle that Aaron was driving and mortified that he had hurt another human being.

As was typical, Aaron had no regrets, saying the accident was not his fault and the woman shouldn't have been there in the first place. What am I missing here? Shouldn't any driver that runs over a person be even the least bit remorseful? Don said it wasn't Aaron's fault and did not even want to place a claim with our insurance company!

Wrong answer!!! I immediately called and filed the claim, so we could at least cover her medical bills for what turned out to be multiple knee surgeries. Years later I heard from a mutual friend that her knee was never the same again.

Chapter 29
Motorcycles Were Not Aaron's Friend

Let's go back to motorcycles – I was absolutely 1000% against Aaron having a motorcycle. I didn't even want him to drive a damn car where he was surrounded by all that metal!

But Don actually encouraged Aaron to learn to ride motorcycles and bought him, not one, but TWO bikes. One was called a 'crotch rocket' and the other was a Harley Davidson. Just because I didn't want it, Don wanted Aaron to have it even more!

Just another example of Don's refusal to acknowledge that his son had some serious mental health issues going on!

The first time Aaron took out the crotch rocket, he drove to my office. I was at lunch away from the office, so he decided to leave. Shortly thereafter, I got a call on my cell phone that Aaron had hit the office's light pole as he was trying to exit the parking lot.

I asked my secretary if he was moving at all or just lying there. She said he wasn't moving, and I asked her to call 911 immediately. By the time I raced back to my office, Aaron had regained consciousness. He had hit the pole so hard that his motorcycle helmet broke in half.

This is a kid who shouldn't be driving a car, much less a motorcycle! My firm instructions/requests/hallucinations were that he absolutely not ride his cycles anywhere in or near the main streets of Yuma. I insisted that he not drive either of them at night, and most important of all, that he not ride them in the city during our winter visitor season. Those poor snowbirds can hardly see a full-sized car in front of them much less a motorcycle!

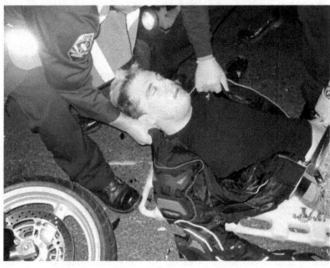

So how and where did this next accident happen? Right smack in the middle of town, at night, in the wintertime. A driver in a full-sized SUV didn't see him and turned left in front of Aaron, as he was barreling up 16th Street faster than the speed of light.

Thank God I wasn't there to see this because the people that witnessed the accident said, in the police report, that there was nothing left of the bike. Mike knew one of the witnesses who said there was no way the motorcyclist could have survived that straight-on hit, judging from the scattered pieces of what was once a crotch rocket.

Fast forward to the hospital where Aaron had a punctured lung, broken ribs and a broken knee. Dr. Peter Cheung saved his life in the emergency room and made sure Aaron was doped up enough to not feel his excruciating pain.

At one point the nursing staff said they were told to remove Aaron's pain patches and all his medication. Aaron was in agony and I was crying and hurting for my son. Torture me anytime, anywhere, but don't let my son suffer as he did.

Don started yelling at the medical staff that he sued hospitals for a living, and someone had better give Aaron back his drugs, NOW! I was not sure threatening the people whom you want to help you was such a good idea, so I quickly called Dr. Cheung's office and explained what had happened. He immediately called the floor and the matter was corrected in mere minutes – even though it felt like a lifetime!

Once Aaron was feeling better, his old habits returned – one of which was his lust for large quantities of food. At one point in time Aaron weighed over 350 pounds – after his bulimia had subsided (of course).

I never saw a kid that could eat SO MUCH! Anytime Aaron was eating at our house, we made sure everyone got their fair share FIRST. Whatever was left over was game on for Aaron!

In Aaron's hospital room, I would order all three daily meals for him while he was recovering. At one point, the kitchen personnel sternly reprimanded me, insisting that all this food I was ordering was only meant for in-hospital patients. His family would have to pay for their own meals. I calmly explained to the lady that all the food I was ordering

WAS just for the one patient! I was surprised the hospital didn't place an excess food surcharge on his final bill!

Not your typical happy American family.

I was there at the hospital 24/7, and it was like 'old home week'. I knew so many of the local doctors and one of the orthopedic surgeons was my next-door neighbor. I never ceased to be amazed that he was also at the hospital 24/7. It would be midnight or 1 in the morning, and he would be there at the nurse's station, happily charting away. Didn't that man ever go home?

Chapter 30
Accident Lawsuit

I don't exactly recall how many years Don pursued Aaron's motorcycle accident lawsuit, but he sued the SUV driver's insurance, the rental car company and even the driver's employer. One of the court rulings went up to the Arizona Supreme Court on appeal (what a surprise) and Don lost that portion of Aaron's case.

What was interesting, years later, was that my attorney brother-in-law (Mike's brother Kent) was attending a conference in Phoenix and the appeal from Aaron's case was actually discussed at the conference. I told Kent that the case was 'hot out of Yuma' and my ex was the protagonist.

It wasn't until several years later that Don agreed to settle Aaron's case. He wanted me to be a witness for the plaintiff's side and I just couldn't do it emotionally, physically or psychologically. I told Don's attorney to tell him that I would agree to be a witness for the DEFENCE because I still held to the belief that Aaron should never have been allowed to drive a car, much less a motorcycle.

The case was settled for a WHOPPING $25,000 the following week! I have no clue or interest in what Don did with his share of the money, but I took my $12,500 and donated most of it to the scholarship fund I had set up in Aaron's name at Arizona Western College. The recipient of that award was majoring in mental health and actually had gone to high school with Aaron and knew him. It was a bittersweet moment, getting to meet her and talk about all her wonderful future plans…and Aaron's sorrowful past!

Chapter 31
Pork Chops MIA!

Early on in our budding relationship, Mike's parents were supposed to come over to our house one evening for a lovely pork chop dinner. Apparently, something happened, and they were unable to make it after all. I learned this after I had already cooked up a 'crapload' of pork chops because I always saved leftovers for Aaron.

After Mike and I had our dinner for two that night, we wrapped up the rest of the chops and stored them in the refrigerator. The next evening, after I got home from work, we decided to eat some of the leftover pork chops for dinner.

I looked in the kitchen refrigerator. Mike looked in the kitchen refrigerator. I looked in the garage refrigerator. Mike looked in the garage refrigerator.

We both shook our heads, totally baffled. Where on earth did that many pork chops disappear to?

After much frustration and puzzlement, we both ran outside so Mike could "dumpster dive" in the garbage can. Maybe they got thrown out by accident the day before? No luck there, either.

After admitting defeat in the search for the missing pork chops Mike and I were both hungry and puzzled. How could that much food disappear into thin air?

No sooner did we say that out loud when it hit us – Aaron!

We called him on his cell phone and casually asked if he had been inside our house earlier that day. And did he know anything about the missing pork chops?

"I was hungry," was Aaron's answer. Mystery solved!!! Mike and I went out to dinner that night.

Mike always said that Aaron was the only person he knew who could open a refrigerator overflowing with food, and say there was nothing there to eat!

Who weighs more – Aaron or Lauren?

Chapter 32
Disability at Age 18
First Time Out

One of my many fears regarding Aaron was what would happen to him if either Don or I, or both of us, bit 'The Big One'. If we were gone, who would take care of him emotionally and financially? We, of course, had a will that provided two legal guardians for our children but what would happen when Aaron turned 18?

Someone recommended that I take him to apply for Supplemental Security Income (SSI) coverage. I was warned that it was close to impossible to obtain it and that I should prepare myself for multiple denials and truckloads of disappointments.

The first thing I was instructed to do was seek a more recent diagnosis from Social Security's designated psychiatrist, Dr. Richard Gunderson. Check! We attended that appointment and I just sat in the waiting room twiddling my thumbs for more than an hour. Where were cell phones when we needed them?

Upon leaving his office we were told he would forward his report to SSI and I should wait to hear back from them. Check!

I had no time frame but...what I did NOT expect was a rather immediate call saying Aaron had been approved.

At first, I was elated that my son would get ACCHSS health insurance and benefits if something happened to us. At that time, insurance agencies refused to cover a child over the age of 18 if they weren't attending school. Then reality set in and hit me like a ton of bricks – was Aaron REALLY that 'bad?' Was he so mentally ill that he would be granted SSI benefits after his very first application?

I was devastated. I broke down and cried uncontrollably because this was yet ANOTHER confirmation that there was something 'really wrong' with my son. When would the world stop reminding me that he had serious mental issues? Enough already!!! Yes, I asked for it but...STOP!!!

Chapter 33
Something Good – Finally!!!

After three very long years of introducing Mike to my friends, family and total strangers as 'My Significant Other', I really wanted him to ask me to marry him. Aaron kept calling him 'Mom's Boyfriend', and I really needed and wanted him to have an actual legal standing in Aaron's life.

If it ever got to the point in my life where I was comatose and dependent on a ventilator, Aaron would pull the plug before the doctors would even ask! Lauren would never let me go and I would languish there forever. So, I decided then and there that I desperately needed for Mike to marry me to save me from the 'great unknown'.

The previous year we had gone on vacation to Tuscany with Lore and Elke. Was I REALLY the only person there that day that thought a romantic proposal on the Palazzo del Vecchio in Florence, Italy was the perfect place for me to say 'YES'?

Apparently not.

Not only was there no proposal forthcoming, but I had to practically beat Mike over the head with a brick to get him to buy me a 'friendship' ring. Geeeez!!!

Back in the states later that year, we had just finished walking through a home and garden show in Scottsdale, Arizona, where we were asked multiple times to fill out index cards with our contact information. No, we were NOT married, so at each booth we had to fill out two separate cards. Yes, I did have a 'significant other'. Yes, we were both living in the same dwelling. No, we had separate bank accounts.

After grousing about how much trouble all this was at the garden show, I mentioned for the millionth time that life would be so much easier if we were married and why didn't Mike clearly see that? So, just like Aaron, with Mike I had to tell him, tell him again and then tell him again what I just told him.

So, guess where Mike FINALLY proposed to me…right then and there in the parking lot of Costco after the garden show!

He turned to me and said, "Do you really want to get married?"

At that point, I did not know Mike had decided that the next time I brought up marriage, he was going to propose. Had I known THAT, I certainly would NOT have brought it up yet again in the Costco parking lot. Go figure!

Family gathering at my 2009 wedding to Michael.

Chapter 34
Las Vegas at Age 21

I really wanted to celebrate Aaron's 21st birthday with a BANG – so where does one go when they are finally legal to gamble? Las Vegas, of course!!!

This was a time when you could fly non-stop from Yuma to Vegas on one of those wiener 'rubber band' planes called Turbo Props. It was only an hour flight and I thought I could handle anything with Aaron for 60 minutes or less. It was just the two of us, of course, since Don never travelled, and Lauren's age precluded her presence.

I arranged for a limousine to pick us up at the McCarran Airport and we arrived at our fancy hotel in style. I wanted to rush out and show Aaron the finer points of blackjack and video poker...but Aaron obviously had a different idea.

After settling in, I left Aaron in the room while I headed to pick up Roni, my twin sister, who lives there. Unbeknownst to me, Aaron went to the hotel bar, picked up a girl and took her back to our room. After their fun, she left...taking all the money in Aaron's wallet with her.

WELL!!! That was the end of that birthday adventure. Instead of chalking it up to a good lesson learned (after all, it was MY money,) Aaron went ballistic. It was about 11 p.m. that same night we had arrived, and Aaron wanted to go back home...right then and there.

He didn't care about the small problem that there were NO flights back to Yuma that evening. He would have to wait until the next day. WRONG ANSWER! He called his dad, who then badgered me all night to stop what I was doing, drop

everything I had planned and drive him home to Yuma NOW!
Like that was going to happen...

I did put him on a plane the next morning and he went home to his dad. Clearly the only person who learned a lesson that night was me – NEVER TAKE AARON OUT OF HIS ENVIRONMENT EVER AGAIN!

Chapter 35
Bulimia and Cutting

As if Aaron did not have enough going on in his life at the tender age of 22, we also had to deal with his newest emotional issue – bulimia. I can assure you from first-hand experience, there is nothing more frightening than to realize your son is actively participating in a potentially life-threatening psychiatric illness of self-induced vomiting.

It is also aggravating to share a lovely lunch or dinner with your son, who immediately excuses himself and rushes off to the bathroom to purge everything he just ate. I honestly think I was the last person on earth to believe Aaron could do this. I just thought he always had to go to the bathroom IMMEDIATELY after every single meal.

How blonde could a mother be???

Aside from the tremendous and as yet unexplained weight loss, we also were dealing with Aaron repeatedly tearing up his esophagus every time he threw up. Many, many trips to the gastroenterologist resulted in every non-specific diagnosis known to man…Only when I heard Aaron tossing his cookies in my kitchen bathroom, did I finally put together the last piece of this puzzle. He was INTENTIONALLY DOING THIS TO HIMSELF!!!

Back, once more, to his treating psychiatrist who desperately tried to help Aaron gain control of his wretched life. I felt as if I was constantly hitting my head against the wall. As soon as I thought we had one issue resolved, a new and more dangerous problem reared its head.

And if that wasn't upsetting enough, I was surprised to learn that Aaron's "cutting" was actually a way to NOT commit suicide. Turns out, it is a bizarre coping mechanism for a mentally ill person who believes it to be the only control he has over his life. How can cutting 'feel good', when there is always blood and scarring to explain? Aaron used to try to get me to understand what a 'sweet release' it was to cut on his arms and wrists. He described it to me as being like an over-inflated balloon getting ready to burst! Each cut released for him some of that 'exploding air'.

What's a confused and desperate mother to do?

Aaron at his lowest weight ever.

Chapter 36
Just Another Overdose

When he was 24, Aaron started spiraling down, down, down right before my very eyes. He no longer took any interest in his personal hygiene, his clothes and body were FILTHY, he was unshaven ALL the time, he actually SMELLED and was getting weirder by the day. I was so frustrated and desperate to help but you can't help someone who doesn't want to be helped. It has to come from within THEM!

And Aaron appeared to be totally comfortable with his chosen life of poverty and squalor. Even though he lived in an apartment with some other guys – he was forever coming over to my house always looking for food and money.

Mike and I came up with a way to help Aaron earn some funds for himself and assist us with Mike's father's hospice care. Aaron was to be Dick Foree's nighttime hired companion. After all, Aaron slept all day long and played video games all night in his own apartment. He, instead, would arrive at Dick's house every evening and play on the new computer we purchased for him.

My husband's dad was 85 years old and, despite suffering congestive heart failure, did not want to experience any extraordinary life saving measures. He just wanted to stay at home, look out his front picture window and slowly succumb to the end of his very special much-loved life.

The local hospice provided Dick's nurses with morphine and other prescription drugs to keep him comfortable during the dying process. Leave it to Aaron to drink BOTH morphine bottles and then call to tell me what he had just done.

I immediately ran over to the house where he was purportedly watching Dick and hauled his buns off to the local hospital emergency room yet another time. I totally lost track as to how many times this particular trek was, because they were all starting to run together in my head.

When I brought the two empty Morphine bottles with me and showed them to the triage nurse, he asked me if the body had been taken to the morgue yet. I said no, the imbiber of the drugs was sitting in their Emergency Department, Room #7. To say the RN was surprised that Aaron was still alive was an understatement!

They pumped Aaron's stomach for the umpteenth time and sent him on his way. No biggie – we were getting soooooo used to it!

Prior to this latest overdose, Aaron had taken some other illegal drug (who could keep track), suffered a severe reaction and was yet again rushed to the Emergency Room. There he was given some kind of charcoal drink to balance out whatever he had digested. Brun Hilda Nurse in Charge said, "You should take him home to let him sleep it off. If you have another problem, just bring him back in."

WRONG ANSWER!

I told her (nicely), that I did not feel comfortable doing that for what I thought were excellent and rational reasons...

1. Aaron arrived at the ER by an ambulance in such a bad state that I was afraid we might have another or different problem after we left.
2. We lived so far out in the county and I didn't want to have to figure out how to do CPR from behind the front wheel while I was rushing Aaron back to the hospital.
3. Lastly, Aaron weighed over 300 pounds! How the hell was I supposed to be able to help him?

When all else fails, start at the top of the food chain and work your way down.

I called the hospital's night supervisor and insisted that they admit him overnight for observation. Once I brought her up to snuff about what he had taken, she not only admitted him to the hospital but also set up an observer to sit with him ALL NIGHT to make sure he didn't stop breathing. The opioid drug he overdosed on was well known for suppressing one's breathing rather unexpectedly.

Luckily, we had a rather uneventful night, but I did not want to take that chance! I am a big fan of Murphy's Law – if I had brought Aaron home you could have bet your bottom dollar, we would have had to rush him back.

Aaron and his cousin Annie.

Chapter 37
Intervention

From: Carol Engler <carolengler@hotmail.com>
Sent: Saturday, January 30, 2010 11:05 AM
To: Tanya Sorrell
Subject: Re: Aaron

Tanya,

I wanted to write you this e-mail to thank you for ALL (and I mean EVERYTHING) you have done for Aaron. I am so impressed with your compassion and professionalism...hard to find in today's world.

As you probably already know, Aaron is changing providers from CPLC to CIA. Dr Jose Martinez, who has known Aaron and his problems since he was 12 years old, deems it necessary at this time for Aaron to be admitted into a psychiatric hospital for intense treatment.

I just wanted to make certain you understood why we are changing horses in the middle of the race. It is not that you and CPLC didn't provide the right services...it's because Aaron never took advantage of them properly. Hopefully Aaron will listen to Dr Martinez now.

Thank you again for everything...and I just have one favor to ask. Is there any way to speed up the process of getting Aaron into 'the system'. He's been to the ER 4 times this month alone, not to mention 2 overdoses so far. I don't know how much longer we will continue to be this lucky!!!

Any assistance or direction you can contribute would be gratefully appreciated!!!

Carol Engler, CRS, GRI
Associate Broker
This is an e-mail to Don Engler and his paralegal Lisa Marie:

From: Carol Engler <carolengler@hotmail.com>
Sent: Tuesday, July 12, 2011 7:03 PM
To: Lisa Marie Catron; LMNOP BEST ONE
Subject: You both can deal with this from now on

I am so delighted with your recent efforts to help Aaron. From now on, you can deal with every aspect of his life. You can deal with getting his meds every month. You can deal with getting him into rehab. You can make all the arrangements to move him into his new apartment and getting the power and internet turned on in your name.

A discussion ahead of time would have been nice...but since you decided to take things into your own hands...you can deal with all of it. Aaron does not have a primary care physician. You get him one. I cancelled his appointment with Dr. Peare. You can deal with that too. And when Aaron dies of an accidental overdose, it will be ALL YOUR FAULT and we will have you to thank.

As far as I am concerned, I hope Aaron lives with you and Marcy at the ranch forever because I am so done with you – you ass hole!!!

Did I sound a wee bit crazed? You bet I was!

Aaron was 25 years old when he sent me this message below:

From: Aaron Engler <aaron_engler@hotmail.com>
Sent: Wednesday, August 24, 2011 9:28 PM
To: Mom
Subject: Hey

How you doing? I am depressed. My life is going nowhere quick.

I am tired of waiting on rehab. They said 2 weeks about 1 and a half months ago.

I don't even want to go anymore. I just want to start my career. Go to college.

Have SOME excitement in my life. Not the boring play computer and watch TV, and do mundane chores for cigarettes every day. I hate my life. I am blessed and lucky I have what I have, I don't deny that.

But people with less lead waaaaaay more exciting and fun-filled lives.

Sweety is almost out of kitty litter. Can you help please?

Love,

-Ace

From: Carol Engler <carolengler@hotmail.com>
Sent: Thursday, January 26, 2012 4:58 PM
To: Lisa Marie Catron
Cc: John Garcia
Subject: Our son

Don, I am very concerned about Aaron. He is slowly going downhill AGAIN and is back to serious drug seeking. His misplaced anger at Dr. Diaz because she would not give him any pain medication is further indicative of his slide backwards.

I have asked John Garcia to speak with you as my attorney in determining what type of ad litem, fiduciary or guardianship needs to be considered for Aaron's continued well-being and future care. I am also concerned that he not be able to get his hands on his motorcycle accident settlement money. He can't even handle the $20 a day I give him for watching my father-in-law.

I suggested to John that he consider being Aaron's 'keeper of the money' so Aaron is guided by some outside third party to buy himself a house, etc. I can absolutely see Aaron getting upset and violent if he thinks either you or I have control of 'HIS' money. Perhaps Aaron having a fulltime caregiver live with him might be an option to consider.

John is in a trial this week, so I do not expect him to contact you until that is completed. I just wanted to give you a heads up.

Carol

A family friend, who knew my never-ending angst and woes over Aaron, told me about a TV program called 'Intervention'. This particular show would arrange a 'come to Jesus meeting' with the addict and his family. They would then provide services at the Betty Ford Treatment Center in order to save the life of the addict.

She suggested that I send them Aaron's story about his 99 ER visits in three months and repeatedly reminded me NOT to get my hopes up. She said that this show gets MILLIONS of requests every week and not to expect to hear from them any time soon.

Well, apparently, I wasn't the only person in America who understood how much Aaron needed some serious help – FAST! I sent in Aaron's story on a Saturday and the show actually contacted me the following Thursday. They were intrigued with his story and wanted me to bring him to the studio for what I presumed was an interview.

I was ecstatic, relieved, absolved and vindicated!!! Someone else in this world thought it was not normal nor socially acceptable for a 25-year-old to make the local ER his home away from home!

My joy, however, was extremely short lived.

When Aaron's father heard about it, he called the show's producer and threatened to sue him and the TV show if they ever had any further contact with HIS SON. Don told them that I was looking for MY 15 minutes of fame because Aaron did NOT really have a drug or alcohol problem.

I wish I had saved the e-mail I sent to Godzilla (Don) at that time. If I left out the expletives, I really had nothing else to say. I do remember the gist of it was I told Don he had just signed his son's death warrant and that not IF, but WHEN, Aaron died from some drug related accident, I wanted Don to know that it was ALL HIS FAULT!!! I was going to hold Don responsible until the day he died, at which time I hoped his was a miserable and painful death.

Why did I sound so upset? It was practically six months from the date of that heated argument that Aaron was killed.

My last picture of Aaron holding his brand-new nephew.

Chapter 38
Aaron's Last Day

Who would have thought Aaron's best day of his life would also be his last? I had arranged for a meeting of all his mental health personnel because I did not feel he was getting the critical services he needed. The participants in that meeting were his psychiatrist, the registered nurse who administered his meds, 'the para-professional', who was a former drug addict and was teaching him life skills, the head of the entire mental health organization, the local dogcatcher and the Pope.

The two-hour meeting was extremely productive and totally exhausting. It is so hard listening objectively to your son being picked apart by a group of people, all trying to help him 'get a life!' The meeting ended with some specific goals outlined and an announcement of some surprising news. Aaron had applied and been admitted to Arizona Western College to become a paramedic. He was also the lucky recipient of a $17,000 Pell Grant. Talk about a HUGE WIN!!!

I was so delighted with the news that I actually went with Aaron to the gas station and filled up his tank to show my excitement for his accomplishment. I was desperate to show him how proud I was of him and a full gas tank seemed the most coveted prize at the moment. Aaron was feeling his oats as well. It appeared he was finally going to have a goal and a real purpose in life. I remember how excited he was to start the path to becoming a paramedic.

I will never forget that day. Aaron had been harassing his primary care doctor for a prescription of a drug – any drug. He finally wore her down and she wrote him an RX for the muscle relaxant, Soma, which he promptly filled.

In the past, I ALWAYS handled what I called 'Aaron's extra-curricular meds'. His Triliptal and other multitude of daily drugs were bubble wrapped so he could take those himself. Anything like Xanax or painkillers were solely administered by me, sometimes as late as two in the morning when Aaron would come pounding on my door telling me he was having a heart attack (at age 25).

I would give him something to help calm down his panic attack and then make him sleep on the living room couch for the rest of the night. I NEVER let him leave my house after taking these kinds of meds.

And just like that – all those years of learning how to deal with his Tourette Syndrome, Bi-Polar Disorder, Asperger's Syndrome, Obsessive Compulsive Disorder, major depression and a diagnosis of being severely mentally ill (SMI) – forever gone in a flash! How could a simple one-vehicle accident be Aaron's final defining moment? And where does a grieving mother go from here?

Chapter 39
That Awful Night

It was Thursday night, April 19, 2012. I had just come home from the office at 7:15 p.m. I was exhausted and starving. On the way home I picked up some Chinese food and was looking forward to a quiet evening home with my husband. I had visions of eating dinner right out of the cartons with chopsticks while watching our favorite TV shows.

Next thing I know, there's a loud pounding on our front door. I hesitated about letting Aaron come in because it was late and everything with him is drawn out and extremely exhausting. He then gives us some cockamamie story about someone stealing his money and whines that he is sooooooo hungry because he couldn't buy groceries.

Sometimes it was just easier to give in to Aaron and, at 7:30 p.m. that night, I was definitely looking for the path of least resistance. I loaded him up with everything I could find in the pantry and refrigerator. There were packages of spaghetti, four bottles of spaghetti sauce, lunch meat, bread, peanut butter and jelly, cookies and snacks and one already opened carton of milk. It broke my heart to see him begging for food. I couldn't bear the thought of him ever going hungry.

Knowing Aaron, I said, "Don't forget to secure that opened milk carton with a seatbelt so it would arrive home safe and sound. And please don't forget to wear your seat belt as well."

I thought he was acting kind of different and weird at the time – but with Aaron, it was impossible to tell. He seemed agitated and spaced out. It nagged at me that he was 'off' but when I asked him if he was all right, he simply said he was tired. (Tell ME about it!) I said to him, "I love you, bunches," and pushed him out the front door.

I changed into my pajamas and crawled into bed, finally getting to eat my now cold Chinese food. I was relieved that Aaron had left, but my gut kept telling me that something was very, very wrong.

I always insisted that Aaron call me after he drove the seven miles to his apartment in town. In my heart of hearts, I knew he had no business driving any automobile, and I always went into panic mode whenever I heard a siren of any kind – ANYWHERE!!! When I did not hear back from him after half an hour, I started calling his cell phone. No answer.

That uneasy gut feeling I had when Aaron left started to grow. I was startled when I received a call from Aaron's cell phone about an hour later. It was the local hospital chaplain, asking me who I was. I told her, "Aaron's mother. Who are you, and why are you using my son's cell phone?"

She told me Aaron was at the ER and calmly asked what I was doing at that particular moment. I told her I was in my pajamas watching television and eating cold Chinese food in bed. She asked if there was anybody home with me who could drive me to the hospital. Duh! Could I have been anymore ignorant of what was about to unfold? I told her that Michael, my husband, and I would be on our way shortly.

Chapter 40
Dead on Arrival

After I hung up from that troubling conversation, Mike and I packed up some books and magazines, grabbed our phone chargers and even gathered some snacks and water on the way out – we had been there and done that so many times that we totally knew the drill. We slowly drove by the crash site exactly 3/10ths of a mile from our front door. There was Aaron's Honda Civic – imbedded in the concrete power pole. We had been through countless drug overdoses with him and two life-threatening motorcycle accidents. Seeing his car ploughed into the light poll barely registered a blip on our radar.

On our way to the hospital I called the nursing director of the ER, asking her to please check and tell me what was going on with Aaron. All I remember is being told something about CPR and that Aaron was not breathing. Well, let me tell you, THAT comment certainly got my attention! That uneasy feeling I had when Aaron left the house had now expanded to proportions I didn't even know existed.

I immediately called Lisa Marie, paralegal for Aaron's dad. I screamed at her to round up Don and get him to the hospital ASAP for yet another 'Aaron accident'. My voice and body started to shake when I told her this one seemed to be serious. I started getting really scared, extremely nauseous and began hyperventilating. What the hell was going on over there and how could Aaron not be breathing???

May you never discover what we learned when we drove to the ER that night. When you arrive at any emergency room and they lead you to a special private and locked room –

TURN AROUND AND RUN AWAY!!! IT IS NOT GOING TO BE GOOD NEWS!!!

We're all sitting there like cattle going to slaughter – my husband and me, Aaron's dad and his girlfriend, Lisa Marie, the head ER nurse and our dearest friends, Sal and Lupe. All of a sudden, the doctor slowly unlocked the door and entered the room.

"I'm sorry," he said very solemnly. Don asked him, "What did you do that you need to apologize to us?"

The doctor said he was very sorry "BECAUSE AARON DID NOT MAKE IT". So, Don, uncomprehending as usual, asked him, "Are you sure?"

The doctor said yes, he was certain.

Chapter 41
How Could This Have Happened?

It took me five years before I could bring myself to read Aaron's lengthy laundry list of medical records from Yuma Regional Medical Center. I was really surprised to see in writing that he had shown up there 99 times over a short three-month period, up to, and including his last and final visit. That's A LOT of drug seeking and the ER doctors noted he was their favorite 'frequent flyer'.

According to the hospital reports, the EMTs were called that night at 7:45 p.m. – just minutes after the accident happened. A witness saw Aaron's vehicle veer off the road and slam headfirst into the solid metal traffic light/power post.

The ambulance was dispatched Code 3 at 7:46 p.m. and arrived at the accident scene a mere six minutes later at 7:52 p.m. Aaron was rushed to the hospital emergency room just nine minutes later.

"This is a 25-year-old male who reportedly was the driver of a car that went at high speed into a power pole," said the ER report. "The patient was not restrained. He was in full arrest on arrival via ambulance and remained in full arrest approximately 15 minutes. Patient is completely unconscious, completely unresponsive. Pupils fixed and dilated on arrival. There are no respirations. There are no pulses. There are no heart tones. The patient has a very large right knee laceration with the patella widely exposed and the knee joint open and likely unstable fracture at the knee joint. There is a large leg laceration and an unstable left distal tibia/fibula fracture."

Aaron's heart refused to 'jump-start', despite being given multiple doses of epinephrine.

"After a total of 15 minutes of CPR with no response, which meant a total of 30 minutes unresponsiveness with asystole (no heartbeat) since the accident and 15 minutes of fixed and dilated pupils, at this point we ceased resuscitation," read the report. "We were not able to make a complete diagnosis of all injuries due to the requirements of doing resuscitation."

Aaron was pronounced dead at 8:30 p.m. on Thursday, April 19, 2012, by Robert Apter, MD.

The report went on to say, "Aaron had been a frequent visitor to the emergency department for apparent drug seeking. He reportedly had taken some Soma for the very first time in the last 24 hours."

Talk about irony and just dumb bad luck – Soma was one of the few drugs Aaron took that was actually legally prescribed. He had just picked up the prescription earlier that day.

Too bad his newly licensed physician did not bother to read, or failed to know, about the contraindications...such as DO NOT PRESCRIBE TO PATIENTS WITH A HISTORY OF DEPRESSION, DRUG OR ALCOHOL ABUSE OR ADDICTION TO DRUGS OR ALCOHOL.

What part of Aaron's addictive personality did she not see or understand?

I never knew that Aaron died the moment of the accident. I always thought he died at the hospital.

I gleaned a small yet bizarre kind of comfort knowing he didn't suffer. He was here one moment – gone forever the next.

Chapter 42
Now What?

Once the doctor walked out of that awful little room, I picked up my cell phone and called my twin sister, Roni. According to her, I simply said, "Aaron is dead." Then silence.

Of course, Roni's first outburst was an ear-shattering "WHAT???" Her husband Bob was with her and asked her what was wrong. When she repeated what I had just told her, he also just yelled, "WHAT!!!"

I could barely breathe at that moment – much less think about my next sentence to her. I simply cried, "Can you PLEASE come to Yuma???"

Roni was already packing her suitcase and on her way. Thank goodness her husband had the good sense to tell her they would head out the following morning. Navigating that wretched road from Las Vegas to Yuma at that time of night didn't sound like such a great idea after all.

Then came the annoying and intrusive barrage of questions from the hospital personnel. "Did I want to identify his body? Was Aaron an organ donor? Did I know if he ever took street drugs?"

NO! I most certainly did NOT want to identify his body. YES, I knew he was an organ donor because I was the one who marked the box for him when he first got his driver's license. YES, I was certain that at some point in time, he had taken illegal street drugs such as meth and crack because he told me so.

My foggy brain wondered why Aaron's fairly healthy albeit obese set of heart, lungs, kidneys, liver and eyes would not be welcomed in a society desperately in need of organ donations. I'll never know but perhaps the lengthy amount of time he was without oxygen precluded him from donating anything but his skin. At least, in the end he was able to help some burn victims.

In the meantime, Don started to call Aaron's sister, Lauren, to tell her what had just happened. I went 'nucking futz' and told Don (not so nicely) that he needed to drive out there and speak with her in person. That was not a phone call I wanted him to make to our daughter who lived nearby.

He left the hospital to go see her and I did not see him again for three years. He never assisted me in contacting people, he refused to help with funeral arrangements and did not give me input on anything. Nada. Zip! Don's parents were buried in the Yuma Cemetery and I would have loved to know if that is where Don wanted Aaron's final resting place to be.

As usual, all the arrangements were left to me to sort.

Lauren had an argument with her husband the previous evening. When she opened the front door and saw her dad that night, the first words that tumbled out of her mouth were, "I told you, we were FINE!" Did she REALLY think he had driven out there at 11 p.m. just to see how she was doing?

I never knew what Don said to Lauren about the accident, but she came barreling down the road to my house that night at warp speed. I was shattered and numb. I could do nothing more than just sit outside with some girlfriends who had just heard what happened (Boy, does tragic news ever travel FAST!) Deep down in my soul I knew this day was coming and yet, I still was not prepared for it. I couldn't cry. I couldn't think. Thank goodness breathing is involuntary because even that was a chore.

My heart was broken into a million pieces. I had failed my son by not watching over him and grabbing his car keys. Was I at fault because I let him try to drive home? Shouldn't I have trusted my gut instinct that something was wrong? Were these doubts and guilt going to hound me for the rest of my life?

My husband of three years was having his own heartache. He had gone to identify the vehicle and said the inside of Aaron's car looked like our refrigerator had exploded inside it. Not only was there spaghetti sauce everywhere, but who would have thought peanut butter and jelly could fly through the air and splatter in such bizarre patterns?

Chapter 43
Somebody Please Help Me!

The day after the accident was an absolute blur...I didn't know where to start, who to call, or what to do. I was just shattered and could barely breathe. I simply crawled under the covers and cried until my twin sister arrived later that morning. I knew she could help me make the necessary arrangements.

I was forced to plan the service myself. Don had walked out of the hospital and yet again out of my life. He wanted nothing to do with me and couldn't emotionally handle anything to do with Aaron.

I wasn't doing much better myself...but someone had to do SOMETHING!

At one point, I staggered out to the kitchen and found my good friend Melinda sitting there. Talk about a whirlwind and blessing all at once! Melinda grabbed my cell phone and started making the necessary calls and lists of things to do. Talk about efficiency! If ever one has a tragedy in their life, they need a Melinda to step in.

She called the funeral home to confirm receipt of Aaron's body and the cremation. She made sure we had food at the house, at all times. She kept track of all the wonderful friends and business associates who sent dozens and dozens of gorgeous flower arrangements and heartfelt notes of sympathy.

Once we decided on a service, she was adamant that my nail technician squeeze me in so my hands would look nice for my goodbye at Aaron's final farewell. Everyone needs a Melinda in her life at times like these.

Two different dear friends from San Diego, Calif. drove to Yuma separately when they heard the horrible news. Both knew me so well – they each stopped to load up on Jewish soul food – bagels and lox, Rugelach, chopped liver, matzo ball soup, etc. at my favorite Jewish delicatessen, DZ Akins.

The owner's son asked them, "What's happening in Yuma? Why are people coming to order food to take all the way to Yuma?"

That next evening was yet another blur. People kept coming and going all day long. One particular heartbreaking moment still hounds me.

Aaron was supposed to go to dinner that Friday night with Joshua, one of his close friends. Apparently that particular friend slipped through the cracks of social media. When he went to Aaron's apartment Friday evening to pick him up, he learned at that time the awful truth of what had happened the evening before.

Joshua drove immediately to my house, sobbing and wailing uncontrollably. When I put my arms around him to console him, I couldn't really tell who was crying harder.

I grabbed my sister and brother-in-law and asked them to console Joshua and the rest of Aaron's friends who were there at the house because I had nothing left in me to give. I was an empty shell of emotion and grief.

I shuffled back to my bedroom and proceeded to cry yet again, uncontrollably. I honestly did not think a human being could produce so many tears.

Was I ever a mess!

Chapter 44
Saying Good Bye to Aaron

I was frantic to come up with an appropriate memorial for Aaron. A Jewish service was out of the question because there were no Rabbis in Yuma. So, what's a Jewish mother to do?

Roni and I had actually gone to a Jewish women's retreat in the San Bernardino, California Mountains the previous October. Maybe I could track down their female Rabbi and ask her to come to Yuma to help another Jewish mother who was desperately in need.

I called someone who called someone who then called someone else. After a few hours of playing 'Telephone Tag' It was suggested that I call Liat Hoffman, the singer/cantor for the annual Jewish ladies' retreat. She wasn't a Rabbi but turned out to be a true savior to me!

I must have sounded so pathetic because she agreed to come to Yuma immediately...even though it was her honeymoon! She and Dan had just gotten married five days ago.

I flew them both from Los Angeles to Yuma on one of our 'rubber band planes'...the 19-passenger Metroliner where you had to give the ticket agent your EXACT weight before boarding the plane. Liat and Dan were expecting a REAL airplane but were gracious enough NOT to toss their cookies on the bumpy flight out...or initially, turn around and run FAR, FAR AWAY!

Prior to their arrival, I arranged for the local casino, located less than a mile from my house, to prepare a honeymoon suite for the newlyweds. Their room was bursting with fresh flowers, food baskets, wine, etc. They could celebrate their honeymoon another time/another place. I needed them MORE!!!

No one in Yuma had ever seen a real Jewish funeral/memorial service. Leave it up to me to show 'em how it's done!

Liat patiently tried to teach me to say Kaddish, the Jewish prayer for the dead. After way too many attempts and painful lessons, she grasped the concept that I could hardly speak English at that time – much less Hebrew. She gracefully gave me a pass on Kaddish and said it at the service for me.

Chapter 45
The Final Goodbye

'Beyond the door there's peace I'm sure
And I know there'll be no more tears in heaven.'

From 'Tears in Heaven' by Eric Clapton.

It is totally PACKED at the chapel. People are standing outside and even up on the stage where extra chairs had to be brought in at the last minute...so many people coming together in one place to show their love and support. Some attendees mistakenly thought Don would be there to attend the service and wanted to support him as well. Little did they know he had no intention of showing up for his own son's funeral. Go figure!

My new husband has the same white hair as Don. If not for the somber occasion, it would have been comical to see all the horse and ranch people in their cowboy hats and boots coming up to Mike to express their condolences...only to find out it was NOT Don.

"We're devastated and barely holding together. We're gonna miss Aaron for a long, long time," says one friend.

"We're here today to say our goodbyes. He was a big impact on my life, and I could sum it up, even though we are now universes apart, he will always live on in our hearts. He will live on in our memories. He will be there with us in our sorrows, and he will be there laughing with us from afar. For you are not gone, Aaron, your soul is immortal, and you are timeless. I love you and will miss you every day and I can't wait to see you again," says another friend.

"I'm here to celebrate Aaron and say how much he's going to be missed," says a third buddy. "And we all know that he had more love than he knew what to do with, and that's probably the most that I'll remember about him."

Salvador Gomez, a dear family friend, opens the service.

"Welcome. Thank you all for coming here today for this celebration of life of Aaron Casey Engler. Even though we only had him for 25 short years, he had a hundred years' worth of love and friendship. Ask anyone here. The first thing they will tell you about Aaron is that he had the biggest heart. He would give you the shirt off his back...the last gallon of gas in his car. Well, maybe not the last gallon at today's prices!

"His apartment on First Avenue had a revolving door for friends and always looked like a refugee camp. Aaron would hear of people who had no place to go and they would end up sleeping on his floors, on his couch, on his ceiling. You could go over there any time of the day and night and you would have to step over all the bodies.

"Aaron ended up attending just about every elementary school in the entire Crane School District before going to Crane Middle School and graduating from Cibola High School. After two serious motorcycle accidents, and many drug overdoses, he had the dream of becoming an EMT, (emergency medical technician) because he saw so much of them!

"Aaron was famous for his enormous appetite. He came, he saw, he ate. If he knew how much food is at Carol and Mike's house right now, he'd probably try to come back and grab all the leftovers!

"Life will never be the same, but that doesn't mean it won't be good again.

"Thank you. And now we'll hear from Vicki who will share some more family stories."

"I first met Carol in 1971 when we were both pretty young, working at The Yuma Daily Sun. So, I've known her family a long time. A lot of you know this, of course, she was a great reporter before she became the world's greatest Realtor.

"When I talked to Carol on Saturday, I had just moved to San Diego, but she asked me to come back and talk a little bit about Aaron. So, here are some stories that I'd like to share with you.

"I think most of you know that Carol has a twin sister named Roni. And she has a son named Tony. And he and his cousin Aaron were born ten weeks apart. So, when Roni and Carol went together to an OB-GYN appointment for Carol, the doctor came in to check on her and saw a very pregnant Roni.

"Baffled – he asked, 'which of the two of you is my patient?'

"Tony's father always called the boys in utero 'Guido and Vito'. The Jewish/Italian mafia. They looked so much alike that when the boys were four years old, Carol and the kids had just driven to Los Angeles to visit Roni and her kids. When Roni saw Aaron racing up the front walkway, she thought it was Tony and mistakenly yelled at him for playing in the front yard…when it was actually Aaron. Can you imagine this? The two mothers just happened to have dressed them in identical fashion that day. Isn't that scary?

"Aaron had such a big heart that any time he saw a homeless person he told his mother that she must buy that man a house. And Carol has that kind of heart too, but not that nice. For those of you who knew Aaron well, you will appreciate his sister's comment upon learning of his passing. When Carol was handed over his package of personal effects, Lauren piped up, 'Well, Aaron is now survived by his cell phone and his nipple and tongue rings.'

"And for those of you who knew Aaron, you knew how he was. Sal was talking about how he liked to raid Carol's and Mike's pantry just about every single day. Where there was food, there was Aaron. And the two of them were synonymous. Carol and Mike's ecosystem will permanently be out of balance from now on.

"Aaron had the greatest imagination and boy, could he tell a story! The day before that fateful Thursday, Aaron told his mom that gypsies had taken his car in the middle of the night, driven it around town, used up all of his gas, and then put the car back in its place. And that's why he needed his mom to fill up his tank.

"Aaron was totally addicted to playing his computer games with his friends. We're all certain his computer and keyboard are trailing after him on his path to Heaven.

"Aaron volunteered for a brief time at the Yuma County Humane Society, except he tried to adopt every animal with which he came into contact. He had to quickly leave that position because his mother just couldn't handle all the ongoing drama that goes with NOT adopting every cat he touched.

"At this time, we're going to acknowledge Aaron's second 'mother-in-command', Lisa Marie. When Aaron's OCD kicked in and Carol couldn't answer Aaron's dozens and dozens of phone calls and texts, all within a 15-minute time frame, he would start harassing our angel, Lisa Marie. When Aaron had overindulged at a bar, the bartenders would call Lisa Marie first to come get him. Aaron would always run – but he could never hide – from that woman.

"Lisa sent this text to Carol this week and it totally describes her relationship with Aaron and his family. 'I am the third twin, the second mom, and the first friend that he could call.' No truer words were ever spoken. Could you ask for a better friend?

"Aaron NEVER said goodbye to anyone without saying 'I love you' and giving them a great big bear hug. Thank God this is the last memory his family has of him.

"Aaron's legacy to Yuma is an awareness of Tourette Syndrome in our schools and local medical community. As a result of the dozens of professionals who helped Aaron stay on track since he was eight years old, his family has set up the A.C.E. (Aaron Casey Engler) Memorial Scholarship to provide financial assistance for students wanting to go into the mental health field. A non-profit account has been set up for this at 1st Bank Yuma.

"And now I'd like you to introduce to you Vivian Klee, who was Aaron's third, fourth and fifth grade teacher at Valley Horizon Elementary School."

"I knew Aaron as a little boy in third grade as part of the three-four-five, multi-age class where students stayed with me for three to four years. We had a little family in those years together overall. We worked well together. And Aaron had challenges to face but, you know, he never seemed bitter or sad about them. I think he enjoyed being with older students and he was a very intelligent and artistic student. I felt like I had the cream of the crop in those years.

"I know that Carol became increasingly active in helping her son and other children with their challenges and continues to do so today. The fact that many kids suffer with various disabilities should help remind us all to be thankful for our many blessings in our own families.

"I know that times are not easy for Carol, Don, and Lauren. I was witness to times in those years when Aaron had to face a difficult mannerism or tic and my heart went out to him. He could be an absolute joy at times…and an absolute terror at others. Oh, those boys in elementary school. I was thankful for the wonderful example set by my older students in the class.

"I lost touch with Aaron in the years that followed but he's a personality I would not forget. Helen Keller once said, 'Death is no more than passing from one room into another. But there's a difference for me, you know, because in that other room, I shall be able to see.' So, I hope and pray that Aaron is also at peace and that having faith in that – Don, Carol, and Lauren can be at peace."

The next speaker is one of Aaron's school administrators.

"My name is Laurie Doering and I worked with Aaron. I'm a principal now and worked with him when he was in elementary school. The poem I'm about to read, when Carol heard it, said those are Aaron's words. So, as I read this to you, I'd like you to think of Aaron saying these words to his family.

'Hey, you guys, don't feel guilty.
It was my time to go.
I can see you're feeling sad.
I can see the tears still flow.
My life's journey ended early.
The path I chose was short.
You all tried your best to change it,
But in the end, it was for me to sort.
I know I caused you sadness.
I know I caused you pain,
But I was captured by these demons.
They wouldn't set me free again.
They took away my freedom.
They took away my choice.
And when they got their hooks in,
You could hear it in my voice.
There were times I tried to fight them.
There was a time I nearly won,
But they came back and overpowered me.
I had nowhere left to run.
I haven't fully left you guys—
I'm closer than you think.
I will be the whisper in the wind,
I will be everywhere you go.
One day you will all forgive me.
One day you will understand.
And when your time on earth is done,
I'll be waiting to hold your hand.'

"Aaron's family would also like to give special thanks to all the people in the mental health field whose monumental job was helping Aaron. You sure had your work cut out for you with this young man and you all rose to the occasion. Thank you for making his last day on earth such a positive one."

Chapter 46
Aaron's Great Send Off

"Hello. My name is Liat Hoffman and I just want to explain who I am and how I got here. Carol, Roni and I are part of a group of Jewish women who get together once a year for a weekend retreat at Camp Mountain Chai in the San Bernardino Mountains in California.

"Carol has asked me to come in from Los Angeles to perform this mitzvah, which is a Hebrew word that means 'good deed'. I will be sharing with you some of the Jewish songs and prayers that are a part of her life and therefore were a part of Aaron's upbringing.

"So, I don't know if any of you have ever been to a Jewish funeral before, but there are certain prayers and songs that are traditionally said, and I'll do my best to try and contextualize everything that we're doing so it is meaningful for you as well.

"I would like to share with you a poem that, when I was hearing about the kind of person that Aaron was, it really struck me as being appropriate. It's called, 'The Measure of a Man'.

'Not, how did he die, but how did he live?

Not, what did he gain, but what did he give?

These are the units to measure the worth a man regardless of birth.

Not what was his station, but had he a heart?

How did he play his God-given part?

Was he ready with the word of good cheer to bring back the smile, to banish a tear?

Not what was his shrine, nor what was his creed,

But had he befriended those really in need?

Not what did the piece in the newspaper say,

But how many were sorry when he passed away?'

"Also, we traditionally read Psalm 23, so I don't know if you have copies of it, but if you know it, feel free to join me saying it in English.

'The Lord is my shepherd; I shall not want.

He maketh me to lie down in green pastures: He leadeth me beside the still waters.

He restoreth my soul: He leadeth me in the paths of righteousness for his name's sake.

Yea, though I walk through the valley of the shadow of death, I will fear no evil: for thou art with me; thy rod and thy staff they comfort me.

Thou preparest a table before me in the presence of mine enemies: thou anointest my head with oil; my cup runneth over.

Surely goodness and mercy shall follow me all the days of my life: and I will dwell in the house of the Lord forever. Amen.'

"So, at this time I would like to invite Aaron's friends to share any stories that you may have of him. The floor is yours, if you wish to say anything."

"Hi. My name is Chris Jackson. Everybody calls me Chief, thanks to Aaron. There's more to the name but it's a bit inappropriate right now. I met Aaron in high school through a friend of mine, Jason Thomas. At first, I didn't really 'get' Aaron and so I never really hung out with him a lot until one time I was in the high school gym class and I noticed that he was there.

"And I was like, 'Oh, I guess I'll go talk to this guy.' We sat down and talked for a while. And he invited me to come over to his house. And I'm standing there, 16 years old, and I'm going to spend the night at some other guy's house. So, the weekend comes by. I'm like, well, I got nothing better to do for the weekend, so I give him a call. And he asks me, 'you know, where the marine base is?' I'm like, 'I just barely moved here so I don't know where anyplace is.'

"And he tells me, 'Well, do you know where Hollywood Video is?' I'm like, 'Yeah, I know where that is.' He said, 'All right. We'll meet up there and we'll rent some games.' So, I go over, we get some games and go to his place. And we're sitting there laughing, having a good time and having fun. And I was starting to get tired and I was falling asleep. I fall asleep early.

"And so, Aaron, the fun guy that he is, goes and hits me with a pillow without knowing that somehow the house telephone accidentally slipped inside his pillow. You know what I'm saying? It was his house phone and he swings it with his whole might and hits me right in the ribs. I wake up, completely freaking out, like, wondering what was that? He's like, 'Don't tell me you're that weak.' I tell him, 'There's something in that pillow.' Then he says, 'Oops, I'm sorry.'

"Ever since that day, we became good friends. I mean, we had fun laughing, joking around. Going around and picking up more of our friends to come over. And his dad would always spend, like, $300 on snacks. They'd be gone within two days. Those were the best times that we ever had. And with Aaron gone – things will be completely different for us. Our friends will move away. And sure, some of us are still stuck behind, but those times back in high school were by far the best times of our lives.

"And I cherish the fact that I knew this guy. He was my brother, my friend. He was my best friend. And you only have people like that once in a lifetime. Thank you."

"My name is Tim. I first met Aaron in the third grade before he went to Valley Horizon. I had transferred in from Las Vegas. Scared, didn't know anyone. Was trembling. Teacher sat me next to him, and I didn't know what was going on. I was just sitting there, trying to keep my focus, keep my mind from wandering and everything. And then from behind I heard, 'Psst, psst.' I'm looking, and then I turn to face him, he's like, 'Hey, yo hablo Espanolo? What?' He's like, 'Exactly.' From then on, we were friends.

"We got into so much trouble together. We did everything from shooting spitballs at our teacher to taking her seating arrangements and hiding them. She tried to separate us and one time she put us each across the room. And Aaron took her paper, crossed out the name of the girl who was sitting there and he wrote 'me'.

"And I remember his last day there before he switched schools. As soon as the bell rang, he threw his arms up in the air, tossed his papers everywhere, and yelled, 'Freedom!!!' I was like, 'Aaron, what's wrong? What's happening? We still have half a year left.' He's like, 'Well, maybe you do, but I got a vacation. They kicked me out!'

"That was clearly the case for us kids back then – vacation was two or three weeks off school for any reason. Eventually, I was reunited with him back in junior high and I also spent a good amount of time with him through high school as well.

"We spent a lot of time together. I worked a lot and the only time I had off was on the weekend. During the weekend, when we hung out we would go to the bars. We'd play pool at Pop-a-Top, you know, drink one, two, six beers sometimes. We were shooting pool and every time you made a ball you would take a drink.

"Well, he was always better than me, so he would always drink a lot more than I did. One time I was sitting there at a table waiting for him. Well, 15, 20 minutes passed by and I had to give up the table. I found him talking to a very attractive bartender. I said, 'Hey, Aaron, what's up? He's like, 'Shh, shh, shh.' Then he said to the bartender, 'Excuse me, miss, I have a question for you. Did you fall from heaven because I have an erection?' I was like, 'Aaron, we got to go, WE GOT TO GO!' Of course, you know, she just rolled her eyes and laughed.

"At some point, I decided to drive him home. We started driving, and he's like, 'Tim, I don't feel so good.' I'm like, 'Why, what's wrong?' The next thing, he vomited all over me. I'm like, 'OK, that's it, we'll go to my place.' So, we go to my place to let him sleep it off. But he wakes up in the middle of the night, wanders into the living room where I had slept on the couch, and he's like, 'Tim.' I'm like, 'What?' He's like, 'What are you doing in my house?' I'm like, 'we're in my apartment; we're not at your house.' He's like, 'Oh, well, that's why all the clothes in the closet didn't fit.'

"I believe one of Aaron's greatest assets was his ability to make people laugh...just the joy he brought people. Sometimes he did it intentionally. Sometimes not. When I first went to the academy, I had no idea what I was doing, and I would call him every month. He gave me so much reassurance in what I was doing, I was able to pass.

"And when I came back, we celebrated. I took him out to Red Lobster. And of course, I wasn't hungry, so I said, 'Hey, you eat whatever you want.' Fourteen plates later and $570, he was full. But that was one of the greatest nights we ever had together, just talking and catching up. In a few months he was gone.

"Another good memory I had of Aaron was when he was sitting down playing on his computer. We had told Don we were going to help him clean up around the house. Don was scheduled to be back in about an hour or so. And we're, like, 'Aaron, Aaron, we gotta clean up. WE GOTTA CLEAN UP!'

"He's like, 'I can't!' He spun around on his chair, put his hands up to his neck and said, 'My duodenum hurts. 'Well, for those of you who don't know, the duodenum is actually quite a bit lower. It connects your intestines to your sphincter.

"So, we just busted out laughing. We looked at him and said, that's not possible. And, without missing a note, he spins around in his chair lightning fast and says 'Oh, yeah, nothing wrong but now my butt hurts. OK, I'll help.' And he helped motivate us to work as he just sat by and watched.

"All right. I don't think any of us will ever be able to forget Aaron. Not only did he help a lot of us when we needed it, he was also there for us in so many different ways that others could not even be remotely close to understanding."

"Hello, my name is Josh Bennett. I'm an old friend of Aaron's. When I first moved to Yuma, I was part of a military family, so I was used to moving around a lot and having to make new friends all the time. So, when I came to Yuma, I was having a hard time. I remember my very first Yuma friend, Jason, introduced me to Aaron.

"He was so very special to all of us. Literally, I don't think I would have had the same high school experience if it weren't for Aaron. He left a big impression on all of our friends.

"One memory I had of Aaron – we used to always go to the library. And granted, we didn't really read anything. Our visits mostly involved us eating Oreos and being really loud (exactly what you're not supposed to do in the library.) We also used to rearrange the World Encyclopedia books.

"I remember the first time I ever got into the vehicle; his parents gave him, a Chevy Tahoe. That thing's a BEAST! He immediately starts playing Rammstein and it's just blasting through the speakers. I've never heard this band before, and it caught me unaware. He's playing this in the school parking lot. And I'm nervous, I'm freaking out. And this security guard just waves him through. He's like, 'Don't worry about it. I do this all the time.' I'm like, 'Wow!'

"Like a lot of friends, we pretty much lived over at the Engler's house. We literally would spend the entire weekend over there at times. We were always having food there and playing video games together. He is definitely going to be missed. Thank you."

One last friend related these tales about Aaron.

"Aaron was always making up imaginary friends to blame for everything that we did. And anything that we did wrong at Mrs. Engler's house or Don's house was completely blamed on these imaginary friends. The names were outrageous. There was actually one time in particular when Mrs. Engler was out of town. We stayed over at her house…the one with the pool and big rock waterfall. One of us got up on top of the waterfall and did a backflip off the top of the waterfall at their house, and part of the rock broke off on top of us.

"I can't remember the name of the guy Aaron said to blame…some guy named Michael, Miguel or something like that.

"The first time we showed up at his mom's house, like, I've never been in a house quite as nice, obviously. And Aaron's just running through this house, like, rampant, just trying to show us every room in this house. He's just like, 'OK, we're going to game here. We're going to sleep here.'

"And even though Aaron showed us where we could sleep, we never really slept. I mean, we were up to five, six o'clock in the morning when the sun came up. And if you fell and passed out, that's where you ended up sleeping. Aaron didn't bother to wake you up. He would literally just step over you and be like, 'Have a nice night, bro, see you tomorrow.' And that was just Aaron. You know, one of the good things about Aaron is when you were at peace or you were happy, Aaron let you be. Aaron let you be who you wanted to be.

"And I think, you know, that was a good trait of Aaron. Aaron never tried to change who you were as a person. Aaron let you be the person that you are, and Aaron loved you for that. Like, every inch of Aaron was happy with who you were. Because, you know, nobody in this world is perfect. And Aaron knew that. And Aaron never, never put you down for that. He never shied away from you because you had an imperfection.

"I remember Chief picking Aaron up and slamming him on the couch. It happens all the time. And the one thing about Aaron is, his imagination was key. Aaron did have probably one of the greatest imaginations that you could probably get out of a child or a man, at that point. I was actually looking at his Facebook page the other day and he still has videos up from, like, YouTube.

"Like, Aaron was always going online looking for the funniest videos he could possibly find. I honestly think Aaron should have had a job researching some of the funniest stuff in the world…even cartoon characters back when we were kids. Like, he would find funny clips and post them, and be like, you guys need to watch this.

"We used to spend every weekend and all summer vacation out at Don's house. Every weekend we had Xboxes, PS3s, like, six computers – all stacked up. And hauling around six computers is not an easy task. My actual first night meeting Aaron was through Josh Thomas. Aaron invites me over and I walk in the house and there's seven guys just standing in the living room just, like, looking at me, like, who's this guy? We got another one here?

"I was actually joking with Mr. Engler a couple of weeks back, like, how did you sleep with seven young men in your house screaming and yelling at each other all night? Like, how did you do it? Because Mr. Engler doesn't live in a very big house. He lives on his ranch. And, like, we're all in the living room and his bedroom is literally, like, right there. Like, how did you do that? He goes, 'I just tuned you guys out.' I was like, there's no way.

"And, I mean, when Aaron would play Halo it was just awful. Like, you could not go two seconds without this kid yelling at somebody. When a player shot him in the head, he swears up and down, it was lag or some other issue. It was, honestly, Aaron's fault. I mean, Aaron was the type of guy that would always play our games which required teamwork. Aaron didn't believe in teamwork. 'I'm going in. I'm dying for you, and then you guys can clean up the mess.' That was Aaron's way with teamwork.

"And I think the one thing about all of us is that we still game to this day. And if there's anything that we'll constantly have with us is the fact that any time we pick up a controller, or a keyboard or, even when we're searching YouTube...Aaron is going to be there because he's kind of our foundation. Without Aaron, we all probably would have just drifted in different directions, honestly.

"So, I think the one thing that Aaron would really love to happen is that we all remain in contact. And the key thing here is don't ever lose yourself. Don't lose who you are as a person or try and change because somebody else wants you to. This is a life lesson. Life is too short for that. It's not worth it. So just remain exactly who you are, who you want to be, and life shouldn't hold you back from anything you want to do. Thank you."

At this point in the memorial, I am dumbfounded at what I just heard from these ARTICULATE boys. All I ever got out of them the past 17 years or so was an unintelligible mumble or grunt. I would never have guessed in a million years how eloquent they could be…especially when it came to describing my son.

Liat returned to the podium to officiate the end of the service. "At this time, I would like to ask all the immediate family members to please stand if they wish to recite Kaddish. The Kaddish is a Hebrew prayer that is recited at the passing of a loved one. It talks about the glorious sanctification of God.

"It doesn't really talk about death in the actual prayer but, the thought is, when the family says this prayer, it helps the soul to basically ascend, overcoming any confusion that it's going through. It's considered to be the duty of the family to say the prayer. So, if you know the prayer, please feel free to say it with me. I'm going to say it on behalf of Carol, who has asked me to do so."

Kaddish was recited.

"So, Carol tried to come up with some of Aaron's favorite music that could possibly be appropriate for this service, but she was not certain that the adults could handle it. Carol chose to have 'Amazing Grace' played instead."

Liat continued, "Itzhak Perlman, the Israeli violinist who suffered from polio in the 1950s, walks on stage with braces on his both legs and leaning on two crutches. He takes his seat and unhinges the clasps on his leg braces, tucking one leg back and extending the other. He lays down his crutches and places the violin under his chin.

"On this occasion, one of his violin strings broke. The audience grew silent, but the violinist did not leave the stage. He signaled the maestro and the orchestra to begin. The violinist played with such power and intensity on only three stings. With just three strings, he modulated, changed, and recomposed the piece in his head. He re-tuned the strings to get different sounds, tuning them upward and downward. The audience screamed in delight, wildly applauding their appreciation. Asked later how he accomplished this feat, the violinist answered, 'It is my task to make music with what remains.'

"We have lost one of our strings. It is now our task to make music every bit as beautiful with what remains."

Liat concluded, "Do not stand at my grave and weep. I am not there. I do not sleep. I am a thousand winds that blow. I am the diamond that glints on the snow. I am the sun on ripened grain. I am the gentle autumn rain. When you awaken in the morning's hush, I am the swift uplifting rush. I am the quiet birds in circling flight. I am the soft starshine at night. Do not stand at my grave and cry. I am not there, I did not die, but live on in you always."

"Thank you all so much for coming. It is truly a mitzvah, a good deed, to support people who are in mourning for someone they love. And the family is so appreciative. Aaron's family invites you all to a reception at The Pumphouse at the end of these services. Thank you all and God bless. Shalom."

Chapter 47
Another Grieving Mother

A day after Aaron died, I read in the newspaper about a mentally ill young man who was shot to death by our local police. My recollection now was that he came out of his house brandishing some kind of sword. Fearing for their lives, the police took the only action they thought was appropriate at the time.

I saw a post on Facebook, asking people to attend a bake sale being organized by this man's family to help pay for his funeral expenses. Having just paid for Aaron's services, I calculated how many cakes and cookies this poor family had to sell in order to bury their son. The number was astronomical.

It just so happened that this family was using the same mortuary. I called the kind gentleman who was so helpful to me and asked him how much it would cost to take care of this poor family's funeral arrangements. I had a small life insurance policy on Aaron and I just knew in my heart he would approve my using that money to help this family.

I took care of all their funeral arrangements and gave the mother a great big hug when we finally met. I just knew that Aaron was smiling down on me.

Chapter 48
Correspondence

I received and sent some of the most heartfelt e-mails of my life shortly after Aaron's passing. Below is just a sampling of the beautiful thoughts that flowed.

From: Carol Engler <carolengler@hotmail.com>
Sent: Sunday, April 22, 2012 7:14 AM
To: Kathy Kehl
Subject: Pls tell Lorna I said thank you for the lovely phone call

I cannot even speak a word to anyone right now without crying uncontrollably so I was unable to take Lorna's lovely call yesterday. Please thank her for me (I didn't have her e-mail address or cell phone number to text) and tell her I am grateful for her thoughts and prayers. Perhaps after the service this Wed. I will be able to catch my breath and speak to the lovely friends I have who are kind enough to call and keep me in their hearts. OK?

From: W. Kent Foree <kent4e@hotmail.com>
Sent: Monday, April 23, 2012 6:16 PM
To: Carol Engler
Subject: Cannot Imagine

I do not know what I want to say, could say, should say, or can say; just know that I feel like I should say something. I choose the subject line 'Cannot Imagine' because in truth I refuse to try and imagine what the loss of one of my children would feel like. Even the brief reference to the possibility makes me shudder. Our great grandmother Poole was sitting

next to our mother during the burial of GGM's daughter our grandmother Phillips and whispered to Mom that, "parents were not meant to bury their children," GGM was in at least her 80s (maybe her 90s) and she was still shaken to the core. Please know that you have my deepest sympathy for your loss.
W. Kent Foree

From: Carol Engler <carolengler@hotmail.com>
Sent: Sunday, May 6, 2012 8:26 AM
To: Lisa Rainbird
Subject: I apologize for this inappropriate method of thank you

I was told e-mail is not an appropriate method of sending a thank you note but every time I sit down to do a hand written card to you, I start to cry and my tears keep smearing the ink. So please understand that this is the only method of communication I am capable of handling right now.

First off, I want to thank you for being such an important part of Aaron's life. You have been there for both of us thru thick and thin and know most of the challenges we have faced for the past 15 years. The first 10 years were GREAT – once those hormones kicked in it was 'bring it on!'

Knowing Aaron is finally at peace brings me comfort…at times. But it is still not enough. I so wanted a better life for him but apparently God had a different plan.

It meant a lot to me having you there at the memorial service and participating as part of my family (which you are.) Please know that I will forever be grateful for all you have ever done for me…

Carol
July 10, 2012 letter to Lisa Rainbird

My dearest Lisa –
I, too, love snail mail. But in this case, I can type faster than I can hand write so you get a combination. An actual

letter from me, typed on my computer. Does that count as a letter?

I just loved your card. Only a few people ask me how I am REALLY doing. So, it took me this long to be able to sit down at my computer without any make up so I can pour out my heart to you (and them) AND cry my eyes out. So, thank you for giving me this opportunity dear friend!

I watched an author on the Colbert Report last week that really hit home. He had just written a book about special needs kids and the profound effect they had on their parents. Mike surprised me one night and said I really needed to see this show that he had thoughtfully recorded for me.

The author spoke of how getting a child different from the 'norm' is like preparing for a vacation in Italy and then having the airplane unexpectedly land in Holland. You're mentally prepared for the gondolas and homemade wine – but there's also beauty in the tulips and windmills.

Changing your expectations does not necessarily mean it has to be a horrible trip.

He spoke of a famous author that lost her special needs son in an accident, and this is what she said while visiting his gravesite. "Here is one flower for the son I thought I wanted, and this other flower for the son I actually had and lost."

After this segment was over, I looked at Mike who was crying his eyes out. It totally shocked me. So, I did what I do best – I joined him in a mutual tear fest. We both cried together and then went to sleep. What a Kodak moment that was!

Did I tell you I started a bereavement group for myself and four other ladies? Hospice provides the counselor and we provide the grief!

All are clients who recently lost loved ones. One woman lost her 31-year-old daughter to uncontrolled diabetes, a young mother lost a set of twins in utero, the third lost her husband in a private plane crash and the fourth one is really sad. She lost her 18-year-old son four years ago in a tragic car accident where the paramedic pronounced him dead at the scene of the accident and left him hanging upside down with his seat belt pretty much strangling his neck. An hour later, when the coroner came to 'officially' pronounce him – HE WAS STILL ALIVE.

Needless to say, by the time they got him to a Phoenix hospital, he died two days later. And she has NEVER started her grieving. Her marriage went down the tubes, she's estranged from her remaining children. This grief group is exactly what she needs.

We have been traveling a lot – I call it running away but my bereavement counselor calls it coping. We cruised to Belize in April for my and Roni's 60th birthday and just got back from Alaska on Sunday. Then I leave this Saturday for Las Vegas for a week.

Hard to believe, Aaron's 26th birthday is coming up, August 1. It seems so long ago and yet I remember everything as if it were just yesterday.

On April 19th of this year, Aaron's friends called me to see how I was doing. That made me cry. Then we held a memorial BBQ for them in his honor and Mike and I made all his favorite foods – ribs, mashed potatoes, guacamole and bread pudding. That, too, made me cry. I ended up running into the bedroom that night and cried myself to sleep – poor Mike had to deal with the aftermath of the dinner (LOL!)

Now I am struggling with what to do with Aaron's ashes. Next month, my sisters are coming out to San Diego to spread our parents' ashes at the dock area where they kept their boat. At first, I thought I should spread Aaron there with them but it just didn't feel right…that too made me cry.

Then Mike and I decided to bury him at The Pumphouse since he wanted me to leave him the house in my will (yea – right. Like that was gonna happen!!!) So that's ultimately what we are going to do when I have the strength to do that. I will see if Lauren and Roni want to join us for that when it's cooler. Meanwhile, Aaron is comfortably sitting in my closet near my shoes where I talk to him every morning.

We are going to Sue's daughter's wedding August 3rd and I know I am going to cry there. I never saw either of my children get married…and now, with Aaron gone, I'll never *get the chance to be the 'mother of the groom'. Why I am letting that bother me – I haven't a clue!!!*

So that's my story and I am sticking to it! When and where can we get together woman???

All my love to you and Kito,

Carol

Chapter 49
Psychic Lynn

I am a person who absolutely believes in the hereafter. A couple of strange incidents further confirmed this belief. The first morning, after Aaron's accident, a strange message appeared on my cell phone coming from Aaron's cell phone number. 'KKKKKK' showed up on my cell phone screen and I almost fainted on the spot! His cell phone was still sitting in my bedroom.

Aaron was ALWAYS texting me that sequence whenever he needed to let me know he safely arrived at his destination or was finished with an appointment.

'Helicopter Mom', was Aaron's name for me because I was ALWAYS hovering over him, trying to keep him safe and relatively happy. And I was amazingly successful at it until April 19th.

The second episode was exactly 30 days to the date of Aaron's passing. I woke up early in the morning and looked at my cell phone. There was yet ANOTHER text from Aaron's phone, asking me if he could come over for breakfast!

That, of course, was his most famous and consistent request for coming over – FOOD!!!

I could barely contain myself about this second text and was baffled as to how it got there on my phone.

Enter Lynn.

Roni and I went to a Las Vegas psychic fair in 2014 and met a medium named Lynn. I just sat down with her and started to cry. I couldn't even utter a word to her. I just sobbed uncontrollably.

She proceeded to tell me that she was being visited by a young man in his 20s 'with lots of unresolved issues'. He wanted me to know how sorry he was for what he put me through all these past years.

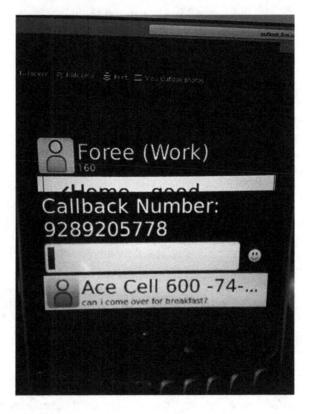

Lynn had my FULL ATTENTION!

At one point, she blurted out, "Aaron, stop it! You're killing me!"

Do you know how many times I said that to Aaron throughout his life? Almost every single day and multiple times on Sundays!

I asked her what happened to him and she closed her eyes and her head dropped to her chest as if she instantly fell asleep. She assured me that Aaron suffered no pain and his soul had left his body instantly due to the blunt force trauma on impact.

Small comfort there…

I met with Lynn again later that same year, and she certainly made me a believer: she knew where I had stored Aaron's remaining personal belongings, i.e. two nipple rings, his watch and the infamous cell phone.

I had asked my friend's 6-foot, 5-inch son to place the box in the back of the top shelf of my closet across from the built-in safe. I had not even told Mike where I had put these items because it never came up in a conversation.

That second session with Lynn blew me away with her statement, "I know where you put Aaron's leftovers"; because that's what HE called them when communicating with Lynn. She proceeded to tell me precisely where all of Aaron's belongings were placed – on the top shelf in the very back of my closet across from the safe.

Now, however did she know that???

Lynn told me that Aaron was perfectly happy up in Heaven helping young children crossover. She was the THIRD psychic to share with me that exact same information.

One was a psychic, I went to see at Madame Laveau's (a former house of ill-repute) during a trip to New Orleans. I didn't say one word to her, but she told me that the person I had just recently lost, was working with young children in Heaven.

A second psychic also told me that Aaron was busy helping young children cross over to the 'other side'.

My twin sister always accompanied me whenever I went to meet with Psychic Lynn. One of my favorite stories is when Roni asked Lynn if our mom and dad were hanging around. Lynn replied, "Your dad asked how you liked his treadmill trick?"

Roni almost fell off her chair!

When our father passed away in February of 2011, Roni became the new owner of his treadmill. One day, all of a sudden, it started running ON ITS OWN ACCORD. Roni walked over to it and tried to flip the switch to off...to no avail.

She then went to pull the plug out of the wall...and noticed that the cord was not even plugged in. AND IT WAS STILL RUNNING ALL ON ITS OWN!

Instead of getting scared, she calmly said, "OK Dad, I understand that you want me to acknowledge that you are here with me. I do."

The minute she said that the treadmill stopped dead in its tracks.

Talk about a Twilight Zone moment!

I made several more visits to Lynn over the next few years. Gradually, I was able to grasp how happy Aaron finally was. I specifically asked him if he had his choice, would he prefer to come back to me or stay where he was. I will never forget his answer.

"I'm not crazy anymore. I am happy here, Mom. Why can't you be?"

Talk about a wake-up call! That was the moment a light bulb went off in my head and I finally understood that Aaron was where he really needed to be after all. No more drama, no more sorrow, no more pain, no more overdoses. For him it WAS a better place.

And I was where I was meant to be – making sure that Aaron's death meant something by helping other people.

Chapter 50
Hoop's House

It was early November 2016. Here I thought I was actually 'over Aaron'. I had ridiculously convinced myself that I was actually used to the holidays without his presence.

Aaron and Me

I was in a happy mood, at a wonderful wine tasting with my sister-in-law, Connie, when I received a surprise call from

John Hooper, asking me if he could name his latest group recovery home after Aaron. I did what I do best. I burst into tears and ran outside. So much for being 'over Aaron!'

I could not contain my delight with this surprise honor!!! And, of course, I couldn't say 'yes' fast enough.

John was one of Aaron's many, many therapists. He actually was one of the three most significant and helpful professionals in his life. John didn't take any crap from ANY of his clients, and he especially kept Aaron walking the straight and narrow. John's favorite saying was, "You can't bullshit a bullshitter!"

John had been a former drug abuser some 20 years earlier. He said his bullshit meter was always on and always right!

I had lost touch with John when he left Yuma and moved to Sierra Vista several years ago. I reconnected with him when he sent out a Facebook post requesting funds for his new business venture, Hoop's House.

John's first group home, Hoop's House, opened in June of 2016 in Sierra Vista, as a non-profit structured recovery home for men coming out of rehab where they could live for 7–9 months, enhancing their sobriety with constant support. These men have to agree to live under house rules including a nighttime curfew, assigned chores, random drug testing, participation in a 12-step program and getting a job.

Residents who receive food stamps are also required to turn them over to ensure the benefits are used for groceries...not sold or traded. When a resident gets a job, he is required to contribute 10% of his net earned income which is placed into a savings account and paid out to him on the successful completion of the program.

To date, Hoop's Houses have had 61 graduates of the program, all who have been integrated back into society.

To say I was nervous when we attended the grand opening of Aaron's House on December 1, 2016 was the understatement of the century!!! I have a picture of me pounding down wine straight out of a bottle the night before!

How was I going to get through this? Would I just burst into tears and then just keep crying my eyes out? Would I be able to speak coherently to the other attendees? Whose idea was this???

Turns out, it was a life changing event for Hooper, his wife Teresa and Yuma County. I was so impressed with the young men who were clean, sober, polite and totally motivated to better their lives that I browbeat John into opening a Yuma house – Aaron's House #2.

By April of 2017, John had secured a house in Yuma that would house nine men. The grand opening was a smashing success – it seems everybody in Yuma knew someone who needed a safe environment in which to stay clean and sober.

Aaron's comment to the psychic was that he was helping more people dead than when he was alive.

If one person can be helped by Aaron's life and this book – then the entire journey will have been worth it.

Or, in Aaron's words – KKKKKK!

Postscript

As of this writing, Aaron's dad Don passed away at the age of 69. He is survived by his 29-year-old daughter, Lauren, 20 horses and 40 cats.

Heaven will never be the same with the two of them up there!